'down the Plains'

Rhea Côté Robbins

2013

Dedication

I dedicate this book to my husband and family who have inspired me to achieve my dream.

Contents

Introduction

This is a book about a female growing up, living in, trying to leave her cultural self behind, and then returning to the Franco-American cultural group which exists in the Northeast, and more specifically in Waterville, Maine. The book addresses what has been asked of me in order to be present to this cultural group of people. As a girl/woman who or how have I been asked to be? What has been asked of me? The book is written from the perspective of a contemporary woman who is also an historical person. The book is also as much about the conditions in which the Franco-American group exists as well as the writing about what it means to be Franco-American and female. This is a book about how we are our historical self while we are in the present. I am more of my past—than I am of the present moment—when it is in the present moment that I now exist. What is, or is not, reflected in my reality and the reality of other Franco-Americans? This book is about the female self and her formation through the many individuals and institutions around her. Through story and cultural filters, the book illustrates family, friends, religion, health, alcoholism, superstitions, art & craft, beliefs, values, song, recipe, story, coming-of-age, generations, motherhood, language, bilingualism, denials, sexuality and what constitutes a cultural individual in a society that will not always allow that person full access or realization to who she is. But she does it anyway.

This book restores the chapters taken from this book to create the book, *Wednesday's Child*, which won the Maine Chapbook Award. *'down the Plains'* represents the complete story of the journey to self.

What A Clever Frenchwoman Says of Americans.—A good many Americans will remember *Madame Olympe Audanarde*, a French woman who sought among us fame and fortune as a lecturer. When home she published a book about us called "*Le* Far West," in which she says: "If not a 'Yankee' by birth or inclination, you will, after a residence of a few months in America, become a victim of a violent spleen—a strange inexpressible discouragement. The word 'business' is forever sounded in your ears, until a great longing takes possession of you to fly far out of this prosaic atmosphere."

She complains of the absence of filial love and genuine family life, but acknowledges that she is lost in admiring wonder at the process of national assimilation which is all the while going on—the annual recasting and fusion of 300,000 or 500,000 emigrants, mostly farmers; mechanics, and adventurers into one free enlightened and powerful people…

—*The Waterville Mail*, Vol. *XXIV*, No. *19*, November 4, 1870

Chapter 1

If Not a Yankee By Birth

We can hold memory—precious or terrifying—a long time in us as a companion with whom we often hold counsel. Discuss the earlier uprooting as a recent event. Examine the tints, the shades. Echoes of the players loom out in brevity and bluntness.

I sit with my morning coffee, alone, the boys are gone to deliver the morning papers in the neighborhood, everyone else is asleep or reading, the memory jabs me. Am I allowed to begin again. Over and over, till I get the pieces in place? The past bellows. Loud, and blows air on the flames of being. The heat presses on me like the hot bed of coals—long seasoned. Being French, Franco-American in Maine.

I am waiting days for the results from the biopsy. Patiently, or at least knowing I am separated from the lump. It is my eighth biopsy. With two bouts of cancer under my belt, breast cancer, radiation, heart ache, doubt assuages, along with reconstruction of my sense of self, I feel lucky to be sitting here.

I am five years old begging the sixteen year-old boys, one my brother, the others his friends, for a drink. After the operation and the ether, I am thirsty. I am in a hospital ward. A porch. Another brother is not far from me because we went into the hospital together, he and I, both of us are in the hospital to have our tonsils out. Bob and I. Twins of a sort. Both of us born in the month of May.

Born of a mother who is a twin. Rita of the Rita and Rhea twins. The *St. Germain* twins from Wallagrass. *Rita* is *ReeTah* when pronounced in French. *Maman* was ReeTAH!

I get my drink because I beg real good. I throw up soon after that.

"We told you. You should not have drunk the water."

My throat is dry and it hurts. The pain passes and somehow we get to eat vanilla ice cream. I embarrass my brother, Bob. Sometimes because I want to torment him in public and other times I am surprised at his anger at me because when no one is looking he is nice to me, but just as soon as people are around he is gruff again. He begrudges me his attentions. So I am in an emotional slingshot. I think I can control the temperature of his benevolence.

"Bob, my throat hurts."

"Shut up, you cry baby," he replies from his status of nine years-old.

"How did you get the ice cream?"

"Ask for it." he commands.

Being older, he always had a better grip on the world around us. He took great pains and pleasure in flaunting his superiority.

When we were older and when I had my cancer, his cancer was much more serious than mine. Of course. I was only having radiation. He had to have radiation and chemo.

"Yours is just a baby cancer," he teased me. He knew how to keep my face off the floor. One challenge from him meant I could not let him win or show me up. It was all he had to say. Some things never change; I was thirty-two and he was thirty-six.

My newspaper delivery boys are back.

"Hurry up in that shower," the older one says.

"Why do I always have to hurry up for him?" my youngest asks. "Maybe I'll just have to lock myself into the bathroom and stay there forever."

Maybe I'll join you I think to myself.

I no longer slept in a crib, but when I went in for a hernia operation at age two or three they put me in a crib that resembled a cage. A stainless steel cage. I remember arguing with the nurse, *maman* and being hurt in my baby pride that I was a big girl who had a big bed at home and now, at the hospital, had to sleep in a crib. I remember distinctly the indignity I felt. All memories darken like old photographs. The walls are green and someone has turned down the lights. There's a dimmer switch somewhere in my mind.

My hospital roommate received presents. I did not. Not at first, and not as many as I would have liked. I wanted everything the other little girl had and I complained. Her *maman* stayed overnight with her. Mine went home. And I was left alone. *Maman* told me I was a "big girl" at age two or three. Even then I was supposed to prove myself and "be tough." Not like the rest of the world which was soft. I remember being in that crib and the feeling of being alone. I remember them telling me I would be all right. I remember being mad. I remember being taken out of the crib. And the relief.

At five, I was back in the hospital for a double hernia operation. Two on each side of my groin. I feel a pain in me, standing there in the hospital lobby, at the tops of my legs, just on the inside curve, in ghost-like quality, which never quite goes away. I am forever standing there wanting to sit down.

I recall the incident so well because it is the time and place where my conscious knowing began. It is the exact pinpoint of time when I woke from a deep, sheltering somnolence; the altered state of innocence in childhood came to a halt that day. I remember it well because I felt the door shut on my childhood self and I felt my apprenticeship into the female begin. My apprenticeship to adulthood began that day. (The wound of being French *avec les améritchains* all around you—being tough in *Franglais*—speech and body language dead giveaways.)

I was discharged from the hospital. My *maman* and dad came to get me and they were arguing in the hospital lobby. Apparently they always argued, but this time it was different because I knew they were arguing. In public. I was anxious to get them home and out of sight of everyone. I was anxious to be out of there.

Arguing in French. Short, clipped insults hurtling around our heads like mortars. Crashing on the shiny, sterile hospital lobby tiles. They didn't seem to care or even know that I was standing there in acute pain. The argument was the more pressing matter. My pleas for them to realize the pain fell on them as an extra, added burden. An aside. My hernia operations after effects were my only weapon to break through to their consciousness. That was when I began to speak in code. That was the time of my knowing.

The first span of the Waterville and Winslow bridge is engaged in the raising process to-day. The others will be coming along in quick succession——if the
river behaves.

—*The Waterville Mail, Vol. XXIV, No. 8, August 19, 1870*

Chapter 2

If The River Behaves

Dreams can be so real that they are more than filaments of us. Stray and striated. I dream a life of exchanges—real and unreal, good and questionable, stark and sparse in its gifts. Gifts with lives of their own attached to them.

I wake to the physical reality of my *mémère's* quilt. It is the second day of its official display in my bedroom on a makeshift quilt rack. I lie there and watch its pineapple pattern vibrate between the white and blue. I picture my *mémère* sewing the quilt at odd moments. Between birthing seventeen children. The quilt's sharp pointed edges converge, jig-jag.

Mémère created order out of chaos and placed the evidence in the cloth. A legacy of the women in our family. To take brokenness and make things whole again.

She was widowed during the depression with a family of eleven children under the age of fifteen. Her sewing needle fed her children. The quilt speaks of a leisure time which did not exist. How she managed to squeeze a quilt out of her life is miracle or miserableness made intangible. Or it could have simply been the work of habit. Hands never idle. The value of the quilt lies in its testimony to her determination of beauty measured by cloth.

I think how the quilt, which was promised to me—as my *maman's* only daughter, came to be mine. In defense of myself against an army of family, I stand on the dignity of my only-daughter status, its legacy bearing power and that my *maman* told me I was to have the quilt.

Actually, there were two quilts I was to have. My *mémère's* and my *maman's*. We would sit on *maman's* bed and talk about the squares in her quilt and what they meant to us. The quilt as a story board. My *mémère's* quilt lay on a shelf in the closet in a heavy plastic bag. My *maman* never displayed her *maman's* quilt because she possessed it in the days before such things were valued as show pieces. Quilts were utility. The women's lives in our family was anything but show.

"When did *maman* die?" my brother asked.

"Almost two years ago," I reply. "In June. It has been almost two years."

All the family, my three brothers and me, the children of him and her, our parents, gather at the funeral home, along with our spouses. Our father, not quite two years after *maman*'s death, passed away that afternoon and we are there to pick his coffin and to make sure he is dressed well in death as he had been in life for other special occasions. The man had his pride. He would buy suits from the best stores in town. To let the world know this working man, this laborer, had good taste.

"When you buy something, always buy the best. It will last you," he often told me. It was advice his *papa* had given him. So he was buried in his best suit.

Somehow my brothers and their wives bestowed on me the task, as an honor, of going back into the house to get his clothes. I went alone.

The house had already become a place of ghosts, of haunts, of echoes. The house, hand built by my father and mother, had already acquired the feeling that someone was never coming back home.

The thought occurred to me to take the quilts, to take them on my first visit to get the clothes. I did not. I wanted the quilts—one my mother had made and the other one my *mémère* had made.

My *mémère*. A woman with seventeen children. One set of twins. One lost through the ice. One died due to accidental poisoning by her own hand in the middle of the night. One deaf because of spinal meningitis. And her quilt. Her quilt she made and ran out of fabric for a last square. She went down to the local store, *"Grenier's,"* and purchased a piece to complete the final square. The quality of the fabric was not the same and so the one square yellowed over time and the rest of the white on the quilt remained white. She had given the quilt to her daughter, my *maman*, to fix the yellowed square. If anyone would fix it, *Rita* would. She was the one who had the determination to get the job done. She never did. And I never will. I like the oddness, the unevenness of the yellowed square.

I have had the quilts for eight years now, I think to myself. This is the first time I displayed *mémère*'s quilt. Other children of my *mémère* want the quilt. Or wanted it. My stealing something, which was already mine, given to me by my *maman* as the only daughter, put an end to questions about who would get the quilts—my *maman*'s and my *mémère*'s. My self-vindication does not stop me from feeling guilty.

In my *mémère*'s family of seventeen children I imagine that solid proofs of a mother's abiding love were scarce due to materialistic poverty. There were other kinds of proofs of love, but only one daughter received the quilt. For reason of repairs to be made. A reason which did not hold water.

There are taboos about stealing from the dead. It took me three tries to get the clothes right for my father to be buried in. I was thinking more of how I could take the quilts. I knew they would not be given to me, but to whoever else had requested them before me. The other relatives disapproved and said everyone should stay out of it and not ask for anything of my parents' estate. Extended family lines and loyalties are blurred at times like these.

I don't often choose clothes for the dead to be buried in. Once when my *maman* died and then, when my father died.

I chose socks with holes in them. Or his shirt was stained. On my third trip back into the house, alone, I took the quilts my *maman* promised me that I could have. I can lie well. I can look so innocent and so pure because I don't often steal quilts from the dead. Only when I am desperate and I know someone else, someone from the other seventeen children of my *mémère* will want the prized pineapple quilt.

I was nervous about the theft of what was mine and I was giddy about what I had done. Thirty-one year old women don't usually go around stealing from the dead. Or the estate of the dead. Or the living relatives of the dead. Or the next of kin. Except I am all of those. The only female in a long line of strong men. It is difficult to be seen in that milieu. Probably, just as difficult to be seen in a family of seventeen. Fighting for space in a family is dirty business. One for which you hope the others can find forgiveness in their hearts.

I was a woman lonely for her *maman* and her *mémère* when I took those quilts. Mistakenly, at thirty-one, I was perceived as a little girl by my brothers who would never allow me my rightful place in the world of decision-making. True, I was given the more homely tasks, but in decisions which involved the salt of life, truth and power, density of being, layers of presence, I was often made invisible and silent. I would not have been heard if I had only spoken my desire, or to remind my brothers what my mother had said to me about the quilts. I knew this and I had to act. At the moment it did not matter to me that I was one in a long line of many who wanted the quilts. The moment I took the quilts I became an individual in my own right. It was one time my place was not to be usurped by another. I would take my chances and I would risk shunning by the family for what I did.

Driving home, I told my husband, "They are in the back." I was sure what I had done showed on my face as I told him.

"What's in the back?" he asked.

"The quilts," I said looking guilty now that I was free from view.

"What quilts?" He looked at me seriously.

"I took the quilts. The ones *maman* said I could have."

I knew there would be some kind of hell to pay, but I did not care. It was the only way I could get them as I was meant to and I knew it. So much for unwritten promises *maman* made to me.

Strangely enough I got to keep the quilts and I'm not quite sure what everyone says about me behind my back, but I felt it was the adult thing to do so that my presence would be felt and real. I was always the youngest and the least heard. It's tough holding up the totem.

There is *mémère*'s quilt. On the rack. In my bedroom and it vibrates with a life much more intense than the patterns in the cloth. My *mémère*'s quilt. I am the daughter of a twin. My *mémère* had seventeen children. Those seventeen children all had children. I have the quilt.

The religious anniversaries of the Free Baptist denomination of New England, which have recently been held in Augusta were full of interest and profit from the commencement to the close of the meeting...The following resolutions on the subject of temperance were adopted:——Resolved, That as a denomination we will hold no fellowship with any person who shall rent any building as a drinking saloon, or tippling shop, and that we will neither admit them to membership with us or to a seat at the table of the Lord if we know it.

—*The Waterville Mail, Vol. XXIV, No. 17, October 21, 1870*

Chapter 3
A Seat at the Table

Cloth is the point at which we all converge. The women of my family, cloth and sewing. We earn our livelihood by sewing. We are self-taught or rather it is in the blood this knowing of needle. The needle and the woman are one. We belong to the cloth. Female-to-female we pass the knowing. *Maman* taught my six-year old daughter to embroider and piece quilts. *Maman* blessed her granddaughter of her only daughter with the needle and the cloth. A ritual passing. I couldn't believe it was happening while I saw it happen. It made me glad beyond expression. I knew something was holy here.

If you are going to be talking about life or living, mostly your own life or living, it is best you do it in a quilt. When I say quilt, I mean patchwork. Quilting comes after you've talked with patches of cloth. After you say what needs to be said, then you quilt over the conversation to hold it down. To make your words earthbound. So that others may know. Or you make yourself a patchwork coat and one for your daughter. Line it with black because some of the words are unsayable. Or some of life is mystery. Not easily understood or known. Like how the baby grows inside of you and how well you knit babies. Somehow, women cannot be held accountable in their knitting when the needles are invisible as they are in the womb.

So the women in my family patch and quilt. We talk in cloth. We say things symmetrically. Or not. Sometimes we say the hard thing. Or the hard thing is said to the women. Mostly, we talk French. Even if we have forgotten the words. The women respond in cloth. As clothes or as quilt. The women scream obsceni-ties, say loving kind words, comic-proportional comment, careful cautions. Playful beggarings. In or about paying attention to what is serious or not. Doling out comfort as well as reprimand. Colors blending power and softness with each butting up of square against square. The separate whisper and yell in crazy or measurably even pattern side-by-side, male and female. Female-to-female or male-to-male: *mémère*, *pépère*, *maman*, *papa*, dad, brother, sister. *Mes frères et les sœurs. Tout ensemble.* In a quilt patchwork of going on about living.

The music plays. Songs go about in our head and we piece the quilt from the box of scraps. Our life's savings and earnings in a cardboard box. If I am frugal, I can save up almost as much as what my *maman* accumulated. "You ought to see how many scraps she has," my *maman* told my father in awe. I guard the scraps and protect them as if they are a kind of gold. In reality they are. They are a recording or progression story of where my life has been.

I take whole cloth woven by invisible hands and machinery, I lay out a pattern, pin it to the cloth, cutting notches. I sew the whole cloth made broken, whole again. Someone I know wears what I sew. As my *maman* before me and my *mémère* before her did. By the sewing machine we live. By the light of the bulb, by the press of the foot pedal, by the whirl of the gears, belts and oil, we clothe our selves, our men, and our children. I place the scraps in a plastic bag, my *maman* would roll hers and tie it with a piece of itself; a few pieces of my *mémère's* exist in the piles. The realities.

Years later, after my *maman* is dead and many, many years after my *mémère* is dead, I take the broken pieces of cloth, the halt and the lame waiting for a messiah to make them whole again, and I cut them into a saving grace of spirit, breathing life into the damned and what once was— lives again. This time, a coat of many colors for me and for my daughter. The daughter who never knew my *mémère*; the daughter who kept my mother company on New Year's Eve in my *maman's* bed of independence against her husband, while *maman* sipped a single, private glass of wine and they watched *The Sound of Music* together. As the wife of an alcoholic, she allowed herself only a glass or two for the entire year on a single night. Even then the two of them were wrapped in the power of quilt. This one a cathedral window quilt *maman* planned out in 1963.

Because my *maman* understood the need for a woman's independence, on that eve of 1982, she kept my daughter company with herself, as my two sons slept in the other room, while I walked places in England she only heard about on the news. She was 62 at the time and she would die the June of the next year. Leaving a quilt. Or two. Which I stole from the empty house the evening my father died a year and a half later.

The Kennebec Baptist Association met at West Waterville last Tuesday afternoon and organized by the choice of Rev. C. Parker of Norridgewock as chairman and Rev. William Clark of Mt. Vernon as clerk...Interesting discussions were had upon various topics, during the three days session, and in response to urgent appeals it was decided to put a colporter into the field, and Rev. Mr. Burrage, Rev. Dr. Wilson and Mr. C. F. Hathaway, of Waterville, were appointed a committee to find the right man for the place and procure the funds for his support...

—*The Waterville Mail, Vol. XXIV, No. 11, September 9, 1870*

Chapter 4

Interesting Discussions Were Had Upon Various Topics

A woman's life is full of interruptions. Broken moments and hours of servitude—voluntary and involuntary. The prayers of sainthood on our breaths or the curses of hell at the heels of what crashes a moment's peace or solitude. The day comes when the woman is faced with herself. She can find no other but her alone in this great big house. She has only to re-begin her life, now. Decide in her later years what it is she wants to do with what is left of her life. Or a woman sits at her sewing machine and runs a few strips of cloth toward her independence on a regular daily basis. I am that woman and my *maman* was that woman as her *maman* was that woman.

My daughter is who she's going to be in this. She pieces cloth like the women who pieced cloth before her, and she pieces music like cloth, giving gifts of musical patchwork.

Other women I know run the cloth through the sewing machine, but that is their factory life's existence. My mother-in-law is one of these women. Thirty-three years of sewing one part or another of men's shirts. The high quality kind. Hathaway shirts at the C.F. Hathaway Shirt Factory on Water Street. Their ads show Grecian, fine-chiseled featured men with impeccable suits and baby-soft cured leather shoes and gloves. Camel's hair long coats. White silk neck scarves. The retirement check of this woman after giving a lifetime to the sewing mill is $137. a month and after six-months of retirement, she no longer qualifies for health insurance. She is forced to buy her own health insurance plan independently. The shirts sell for $50 to upwards of $70 apiece in the men's shops which sell quality clothing.

I was destined for the men's shirt factory mill. As so many of my neighbor women were destined.

I do not pride myself on the escape. I always meant to come back and tell you of the different kind of piecing my women, women of my French culture and women of other cultures have had as a way of life. A serious way of life; an honorable employment. Hard-working people. *Ça travaillait forte c'monde là.*

I have heard stories all my life of these women in the shirt factory. A revolving door sort of place. A place where there are opportunities to go home and have a nervous breakdown, a baby, a change of heart and mind, only to come back later on when you can. A place which requires the women to buy their own scissors, an essential tool of the trade, like the master craftspersons they are. A shirt begins from the top of the building where it is cut and proceeds down through the floors, stops long enough at each block to have the whole-made-pieces, pieced to whole again, on to the basement for final inspection, packaging, and shipping. The building is brick-oven hot in the summer with women fainting from the heat, machine-warm in winter, sitting on the edge of the river which sometimes, in Spring, floods the parking lot. Work starts at 6:00 A.M. in summer to allow the women to leave early before the building heats up beyond human endurance. Or so that is how the process has evolved over the years. Voted in by the union.

Negotiating a day off is reason for a visit to the office and being made to cry by the boss. On the other hand, if on any given day there is not enough work for a worker to stay, then they are sent home without pay or apology. The hazards of the factory.

Recently the women punched out and were paid their averages in order to do inventory. A momentary pause or release from the mesmerization of the machines. To perform the yearly counting ritual. How are we doing? On a good day, an expert, old hand at this can sew up to 120 dozen. Which makes for good pay. Careful not to upset the bosses, mostly men. The women bring batch tickets home in their purses so their averages will remain average. The company figures that if you sew above your averages then the job is too easy for you. If you get too good on a job, they'll move you to another job. One you have to learn how to do from the beginning. A self-destroying type of self-governance to keep your averages, average. You can't be too good on the job, or else.

Of course, bringing batch tickets home in your purse is not allowed. But they do it anyway. Living on the edge caught between performance levels of sewing too fast, too good and the fear of being fired. Breaking company unwritten and written policy. A woman apart from all the women, sewing on her collar stays, pockets, collars, cuffs, bands, shirt fronts and backs. Yes, women's lives are full of interruptions, but more importantly, a woman's life is knowing how to put those interruptions into a coherent whole.

Every family needs to keep in the house something that will cure headache, toothache, ague pain, lameness, bruises, cramps and other kinds of pain and suffering, and what is there so good as Renne's Pain Killing Magic Oil. Try it. Sold by I. H. Low & Co.

—*The Waterville Mail, Vol. XXIV, No. 18, October 28, 1870*

Chapter 5

Something That Will Cure

When I had cancer the second time, the time I lost my left breast, I lived far away from the shirt factory by then. I know women in my family who work there, but I had been gone from the sight of the mill, within walking distance from my home for many years. There are many women, maybe 500 or so who work in what I fondly call "her mill." There is the male equivalent in my home-town of "his mill." I often refer to "his and her mills" when I speak or think of my people. I had been gone from "her mill," and the women who work there are of my people—the French-speaking or French cultural people whose ancestors originated 400 years before from France.

Ironically, the Statue of Liberty, given to the United States from France as a gift symbolizing freedom was not necessarily meant for the French immigrants who came to the U.S. via the land bridge from Canada. For the French people immigrating to the U.S. in the 1600's, the statue should be relocated somewhere in the St. Lawrence. There the French would also need a translation of "give me your hungry and your poor..."

The women who work in the mill, and whose aspirations have much to do with the dominant society under which their ancestors came to rest and be employed by, still speak the language of their ancestors. Or if not, it is apparent in their demeanor, gesture, and their esprit de corps. Body language. It speaks to me. That and the magic the women weave over the years. The superstitions I grew up with. Holy Water sprinkled on the windows during a rainstorm to prevent the lightning from striking. Are we going to have a field day tomorrow? Put your Virgin Marys in your windows so we will have a sunny day. Talisman of luck; omens of fortune—good or bad—ran in close existence to reality. Hat on the bed, eating utensils falling on the floor, itchy noses, open umbrellas in the house, spilt salt and more. The secular were not as mystical or as powerful as the sacred keepers of ourselves, our children and our men. Scapulars were the death-defying cloth medals on string which could keep you from drowning in the mighty Kennebec, for Christ's sake.

I had been gone from the mill for many years when I had cancer the second time and I lost my left breast. News travels fast that travels unofficially. Among the women workers was a sacred woman; a holy woman. A woman of God. I never saw her face and she has never seen mine. She reaches across the distances I have traveled and she calls me to the banks of the river once again. Her hand reaches out to bring me home across a divide no mile could ever measure. She, in the language of my people, in our prayers, from my deepest memory, my oldest self—older than my lifetime— reaches out to me in my ordeal of breast cancer and sends me a scapular medal and murmurings in the French language prayers which can evoke providential personal assistance. Through the grapevine of women, this holy woman gave to my mother-in-law to give to me, her gift of scapular medal which I hung on my bedpost where it remains to this day. I have never set foot in the mill a moment of my life other than to shop in the "seconds" store, and it does not matter that I live far away in body, I can be recalled.

A woman has been admitted to the Typographical Union of Washington—
and yet the sun continues to rise and set as before.

—The Waterville Mail, Vol. XXIV, No. 13, September 23, 1870

Chapter 6

And Yet The Sun Continues To Rise

I'm pregnant. I'm having a book. Women from my culture rarely have books born out of them. This is one woman who wants very badly to have this book.

Like the Virgin of window sills, I want an impregnation of mythical proportions. A new myth to set me free. Mostly from myself. My self-hatred. I am a Wednesday's child. You know the rhyme? Wednesday's child is full of woe. That's me. Except, I don't know it or I never did or if I did, it didn't matter. It was more fun running the lines. Skirting the edges. In the cemetery with my brother and Jerry, Ron and Ricky. One of them is dead now and I can never remember which. Died in a car accident. Blown off the road in a Volkswagen beetle. I can't bring my childhood friend back, though I wish I could. It did not seem possible one of the perpetually young could die like that.

We sit around in the sandbox and make towns; new towns every day, visit each other, step on someone's house by accident—kill the whole family inside. Have to make a new house. One of them eats bugs, raw.

The sand box is at Jerry-Ron-and-Ricky's house under some kind of spring flowering tree. I, and my three friends, stand at my house to have our picture taken when I am four by the newly planted lilac bush. We are forever there beside the bush, measuring our mutual growth over the years. Except the lilac grew much taller than any of us ever dreamed it would and left us all behind to scatter to the four winds. We can't all be Wednesday's child. Some of us have to be born on the rest of the days of the week.

My own children are a Friday's child, a Sunday's child and a Tuesday's child. Those are good days. Wednesday's children have a long row to hoe. Or many seeds to plant. When I was four, maybe three, my job was to put the corn seed in the ground after my father had formed the row. Being low to the ground, I would then cover the seed; I would rather be playing. Or running around with Jerry-Ron-and-Ricky. Play in the sandbox, make towns, crush people, have floods, accidents, visit the sand people's homes, eat mud-pie pies make-believe. Leave mad when I couldn't get my way. Throw sand ball bombs. Get sick at the sight of Ricky eating bugs. I could not eat onions for years remembering Ricky chewing on the bugs he'd find and crunch. The feel of the onion under my teeth sounded a lot like the crunch of the bugs Ricky chewed. It's awful. I can't ever remember which of my childhood daily companions died in a car accident. I wonder if he was a Wednesday's child, too?

"Roneka, The Forest Queen" is the title of an original operetta written by a young lady of this village, to be performed at Town Hall on Friday evening of next week. The parts will all be taken by young ladies—among whom will be musical talent that promises an attractive exhibition.

—The Waterville Mail, Vol. XXIV, No. 20, November 11, 1870

Chapter 7

An Attractive Exhibition

Wednesday's children are those who are born in the middle of the week. Somewhere in the middle of it all. Wednesday's children get it from both ends. Sometimes it is something good and sometimes it is something not so good. They used to say Wednesday is Prince Spaghetti Day. That was for the Italians. There were not too many Italians in the town I grew up in. The French people ate spaghetti anyway. Too much, according to my older brother. He refuses to eat *"spaghet"* to this day. When I married I learned to make spaghetti so good, people told me I must have Italian somewhere in me. What I wanted to do, was to make an economical meal which reminded you of wealth. Of nights in Italy which came through the sauce. Sometimes, I'd bake an Italian bread, too. Mostly, I made white bread. Four loaves every week when I was first married. It would cost me ten cents a loaf to make. Friends would come over and hope it was bread baking day. You do something that often, for a long time, you get good at it and then the heart goes out of it and the skill goes somewhere back there in memory like a great being or presence it is. Some days, I let my bread baking come back to me. I wonder who I used to be and what I was like back then. Before I had my children, or before people died, or before I had cancer. Nobody who was close to me was dead yet. I think of the time when I began to sort things out for myself. Coming from where I came and going to where I am going.

I step away from my French beginning often. From my Franco-American neighborhood. I am on a search for a classical existence. One of white lights **only** on the Christmas tree. I arm myself to the teeth in hopes of leaving myself behind. The one who lives in a neighborhood of French speaking peoples.

Neighborhood as concrete sidewalks sloping sideways on the way to school. Fighting who would walk next to whom. I was always fighting for the middle. The middle meant you could hear everything that was said and that you could be the one next to the popular girl, which was not the one in the middle, but the one on the end and the other girl on the other end had to be kept away from the popular girl.

We played a dodge game when we walked home. A fight for space or place where our importance in the social order fell in step with who walked closest to the popular girl. I was the highest in the social order because of how I figured out to walk in the middle. Until I told no one, my status walking home was quite high. I fought for the middle spot and we would walk home jostling each other to maintain the horizontal queen of the sidewalk. Popularity came to a person by a special benediction from God. No one needed to point out this special benediction from God because we could feel the dispensation in the girl. She had the longest, dirtiest finger nails on a little girl I had ever seen. Her nails shocked me, but her sense of person was so fine that we only mentioned the nails once amongst ourselves and that was years later when she had discovered the miracle of the fingernail file. My own nails were kept clipped short and bleeding at all times. I practiced several forms of cannibalism and self-destruction. I also ate my brown paper bag book cover off my books and the mohair yarn from Gabrielle's newly knitted beret. I gutted pencils and used their erasers as chewing gum. The nun would say, "Spit out the chewing gum. And stay after school tonight."

I'd spew chewed eraser into the trash and go home on time.

The ritual of biting my nails to the quick and all the skin surrounding the nails was a point of pride and a show of extreme I-don't-care. Biting the inside of my mouth seconded the air of nonchalance and furthermore ensured the middle ground I had acquired for myself on the sidewalk morning, noon and night. I maintained a aura of I am tough and don't you mess with me by several female chest puffing rituals that I personally devised. Some were taken from my brothers and family habits which I adapted and implemented with huge success. In the land of parochial school in order to survive you had to have a gimmick. My way of rising above the Christian, Catholic crowd was to refuse to run in any popularity contest when I failed to break through "Red Rover, Red Rover send Rhea right over" and was laughed out of the game and when the cheese began to smell when we played "Farmer in the Dell."

"Farmer in the Hell," I think to myself now.

Compared to Catholic parochial school, my sandbox guy friends were nice. At least with them we could decide on a game or a way of being. Catholic school children playing Monday through Friday on the Sunday church parking lot, because the church was on third floor over the school, develop a hardness of being which does not allow for touch of the humane. We live a complicated system of reward and punishments. Reward is singular because that came only at the end of the year; punishments were daily. Mostly for who or what you were. Ethnic cleansing in the case of parochial school meant to dehumanize you to the point of prayer—to be released from this private hell. So, in order to survive, you develop tactics which are not healthy. The abuse begun in the classroom, continued outside in the yard. Every thing was divided according to sex—gender. Boys on one side; girls on the other. A crack in the sidewalk determines your sex. One step over the line while the patrolling nun's back was turned made you a hero or got you a punishment. We all knew we were sinning when we stepped over the crack to the boy's side, but we sinned anyway. If you were caught stepping over the line you got either a look of reprimand which you immediately mimicked when the nun's back was turned on her Angelus patrol or you had the opportunity to stand with your face pressed against brick for the rest of the recess.

One year, due to our continued unpious playing during the ringing of the Angelus, the nuns came up with a idea. At the strike of noon when the church sexton faithfully rang the Angelus, we were to cease our pagan playing—stop all motion—and pray. A short prayer, mind you, but with a mindfulness to our dear God—*nôtre bon Dieu*. The message was delivered en masse to the entire school. Tomorrow when *M. Thibodeau* rings the bells, stop your playing, and pray. The nuns thought they had infiltrated the yard at last. Our indoctrination would be complete. The bells rang, the children stopped, but it is how we stopped that forced the nuns to rescind their request and to tell us to continue playing at the ringing of the Angelus.

As the bells rang, we froze in motion however we were. Our grotesqueries grew with each passing day. We devised a contest to see who could come up with the best deformed body pose to pray in. I often wonder at the tableau we presented to the surrounding apartment dwellers. At the stroke of noon the entire school yard of 300 or more children would deaden to a silence and freeze in motion as if time frozen. When the bells seized their ringing, action would resume with the feeling we had never dropped a second. Crash the boy into the wall, jump the rope, tag the boy inches away just unthawed, twirl the girl, bounce the ball, roll the marble. The anticipation before the bells rang grew to a pitch and volume of scream, delight and decadence to match Mardi Gras. The nuns removed the request when they saw their only recourse was to jail us all. The Angelus rang over the heads of playing, running, jumping, screaming unhypocritical children for the rest of my stay at Notre Dame School. Give a good Catholic child a religious artifact and we could undo its mystification or power in five minutes. We became expert at deflecting punishment.

Forced to eat the lunch? Throw it up. Go to confession too often? Make up some sins. Splash the holy water too fast with your fingers and before you know it the font is empty. In later years, go into the church during recess and light all the candles or blow them out depending on how you feel. All as a matter of sabotage and undoing the too strict ritual placed on ordinary children who were expected to be at all times—temples of God. Temples of Doom.

A match game of base ball between the Lightfoots of West Waterville and the Conglomerates of Waterville was played Saturday afternoon in the University park—the Conglomerates winning 31 to 16.

—*The Waterville Mail, Vol. XXIV, No. 12, September 16, 1870*

Chapter 8

A Match Game

Bid's boys and me. I am dressed ready to play. It's another day of summer. It takes so long to get my hair combed. To get the pony tail tight enough to hold all day. Pull and pull harder, comb crash, pull some more; my scalp is not sensitive to *maman's* hard combing. Finally she rounds the elastic around and around puts in two barrettes. *"t' Chan,"* she says, "you can go, you wiggle worm."

Finally, I am let loose! The air is morning fresh and the dew is wet on my Keds Red Ball sneakers. I can only wear sneakers in the summer. So many rules. "Bad for your feet," they'd say. "Ruin your feet if you wear sneakers all the time."

I take the hill on which the house sits. In the gardens, deep, black, wet, moist soils live, but around the house sandy loam lies beneath the grass. I love the feeling of sifting the dirt between my fingers. I sit in the dirt, content to sift it. I let it flow through my fingers. If the dirt is extra special, I put a handful in my pocket and touch its softness all day. It feels like brown flour between the fingertips.

I play in the bag of flour when *maman* is baking. I sit with both arms in the bag up to my elbows. I plunge my arms into the twenty-five pound bag of flour, my face peers into the blue-lined, paper flour bag reveling in the sight of the feel; the hairs on my arms emerge white with flour. "I'm a ghost," I tell *maman*. "Get out of my flour," she chides. I don't move. Because time is non-existent, I worship and I play with the flour rubbing it between my fingertips. I love the softness of the flour; I talk to myself, low under my breath. I tell myself how the flour feels as I burrow deep into the flour bag. I make up a commercial.

"Fluffy, fluffy Flour. Good for baking cookies, pies and cakes for your boys and girls. Husbands, too. Good enough to bake your favorite recipe and ours— Burnt Sugar Cake with Burnt Sugar Frosting. The recipe is on the bag. So moms, buy Fluffy, fluffy Flour the next time you bake. And feel the softness."

I am friends with the three boys next door. "Bid and her boys," *maman* would say. *Maman* had her girl. Bid always wanted a girl and she had seven boys. Every time Bid got pregnant we'd all wait for her girl. When another boy was born after five boys, Bid would cry. But she'd cry only for a short while, have a fight with her husband, go for a fast car ride, come home and love that boy like he was her first.

All those boys and living in the French neighborhood, she would give her boys names that made my *maman* wonder where she ever got names like that. English names. Short names. One-syllable names. "Boy, don't I like that name," Bid would laugh. She always laughed a deep, throaty laugh. "Ha. Ha. Ha." We'd all laugh with her and then we'd all pretend to understand the strange sounding names she'd call her boys and we'd go along with her. After all, she never got her girl. *Maman* would say: "That's Bid. Bid can be funny sometimes." Except *maman* didn't mean Bid told jokes. Funny meant odd; funny meant not French.

Bid was odd—not French, but she and *maman* got along. They had a mother's agreement. They would never fight because of the kids they said. If Bid ever had enough of me or if I was bad and if *maman* ever had enough of Bid's boys— "Ship her home," or "Ship 'em home," they'd say. It was a good agreement they agreed. So, sometimes I get shipped.

I spend a lot of time with Bid's boys. At their house. They have a metal swing set with a slide. I have a single swing, homemade, with a wooden seat on yellow and black rope. My father always makes me a swing every spring and hangs it on the two-by-four straddled between two telephone poles. I can swing high, but I have to swing alone. With Bid's boys on their metal swing set, we can all swing, teeter or slide. We can almost tip the whole thing over, too. If we swing high enough. They have a sprinkler attachment and I have a garden hose with holes all along it.

But, most important, they have a sandbox. We don't limit ourselves to the sandbox, me and Bid's boys, because we know all the great dirt places around. We have the run of the neighborhood. Next to the sandbox, our favorite dirt place is in a gulch dug out of a hill in which *bon homme* and *bonne femme Chamberlain's* house sits. *Bon homme*, which is said as if it is one word pronounced as *bonhomme*, means to *us* M. Chamberlain, and *bonnefemme Chamberlain*, his wife, are good people to let us play in their flour dirt.

Bonnefemme Chamberlain is sick and often sleeps. We work our play in and around her naps. We ask permission to play quiet beside their house in their dirt. We knock at their door to ask. They tell us yes or maybe not today. If we are too loud and get into a fight over who owns what dirt, *bonhomme* or *bonnefemme* tell us we have to go home to play.

In the sandbox there are rules. Corners. Times of day when we can play, usually by nine or even earlier if the sand is dried enough by the morning sun. The sandbox is in the shadow of the lilac bush grown tall and selfish.

The sandbox is our common domain. There are faces and lives to the people in our sand houses. Dirt reigns king. Into it we work our lives and tomorrow we begin all brand new. New lives, new jobs, new houses, new towns, and new roads.

When I come across the field kept mown or a path worn through with our daily traffic, I find Bid's boys started without me. I step in the sandbox over the wooden sides and I step into a magic place. We are imperious in our play. Held tight by the rules, we determine the lives of our sand people.

"You can visit me in my house," one of Bid's boys say. "No, you come see me," I tell him, "then I'll come to your house." "My man—it's always *my man*—is going to work now, so you can't come over. Bid's boy drives a car around the sandbox. "He's back. So you can come over now." "I'm stuck. Come get me out." "Help me build my roads." "No, I'm busy building mine. I'll be over when I'm done. Okay. I can help you now."

Sandbox play effects what I eat. One of Bid's boys east spiders and bugs raw. Dark hair, flashing eyes, the youngest of my three friends. Eating bugs is his way of being boss or best. Sometimes if he wants the sandbox to himself, he finds a juicy spider and chomps down on it. "Look at me!" Bid's boy says. We look and teeth crunch down on the spider; legs and body crushed as he relishes every bite.

Or Bid's boy holds a beetle high over his head, dangles the beetle by a leg, slowly lowers the beetle into his mouth. "Mmm. Mmm. Beetles are my favorite," he says. Our bellies revolt. I go home.

My *maman* has made soup for lunch. Spaghetti soup with onions floating in it. I sit to eat and I pick out every flake of onion, still crunchy. Crunchy like a spider's or beetles body. I make a small pile of transparent onions on the table beside my bowl. *Maman* says, "You never eat your onions." "I don't like the crunch," I tell her. I never tell her why. I'm thirty-two years old before I eat an onion on purpose.

My daughter, who never met Bid's boy, also refuses to eat onions because of the crunch. "You never eat your onions," I tell her. "I hate the feel of the onions when I bite on them," she tells me at three, four and five years old. Someday, I tell myself, I'll tell my daughter the story of Bid's boy and why she won't eat onions. Onions that crunch like bug bodies.

The bridge is making steady progress in its way across the Kennebec. The first pier and the second span are advancing together, and to those who know something about the matter the enterprise looks well.

—*The Waterville Mail, Vol. XXIV, No. 10, September 2, 1870*

Chapter 9

To Those Who Know Something About The Matter

It is not easy to lose your left breast. I cannot imagine it is easy to lose your right one either. You grow these things and then you get used to them. My breasts started to grow when I was in the third grade. Baby breast buds were on my chest. Nipples protruded. Hernias do that, too. I was a three time survivor of hernias. The hernia in my groin would protrude and they would push it back in. I'd get another hernia and they'd say, "Oh, oh. Here we go again." They took me to the doctor. Told me to take off my clothes except your panties and told me to lay up on the wooden table with a little padding on it and covered in leather. I was given a sheet to cover up with. The nurse was kind. Fast when she moved. Friendly. French. She knew our family. She was an old classmate of my oldest brother.

"He was always such a tease," she said. She looked like she liked him.

"Ah, bien, chère, assis-toé icitte. As-tu frette, chère?"

I like her. The doctor too, I thought. In the beginning. First there was the tonsil operation. Then there was the double hernias. He was friendly. His examination hands were kind. And he always asked, "Does this hurt?" Just to please him, even if it did hurt, I nodded no. And then in my child's brain I wondered what it was supposed to feel like. So when I went back for a final check-up and he asked, "Does this hurt," I said "yes." Just to see what he meant by hurt. I was confused.

"It hurt a little, but only when you press hard like you just did, and then if you don't press, well, it feels OK."

He seemed impatient. And disappointed. I had been such a tough little girl. Tough. I resented it. I wanted to whine and cry like everyone around me and I couldn't. I had to be tough. Or else.

My breast buds looked like a hernia to me. A double hernia, but this time on my chest. I was upset to think I would have to go back to the hospital to be operated on again. I went down cellar where my mother was doing her wash.

"I think I have another hernia," I told her. It was always "another hernia."

"What!" she sounded puzzled. Distracted.

"I have two bumps on my stomach," I hesitated.

"Show me."

So I lifted my shirt and sure enough, there were two hernias growing out of my chest.

"You ninny, those aren't hernias," she said in an impatient tone. "Those are your breasts starting to grow." I had caught her at a busy time.

My eyes grew wide. I was puffed up with pride. MY BREASTS?! I wanted to tell the whole world. I called my friend Jacquie to meet me in the snow fort. I had a great, big secret I wanted to tell her.

I put on my coat, my leggings, my boots, my hat, my mittens and I went outside to visit with Jacquie for a few minutes before we had to eat supper.

She came a few minutes later. Jacquie was a year older than me. A girl had finally moved into the neighborhood. Her family was renting from my family. She was poor and she was mean. She was jealous of me. She was skinny, loud, and she bragged about her daddy. Her mother had divorced the man because he was an alcoholic. Her mother had remarried a new man. One of the foremen at the women's shirt factory. Soft spoken beer drinker. He beat her mother like the last husband did. Only once and then her mother hit her second husband harder and threatened that she would kick him out too, so he stopped beating his wife. But we weren't supposed to know all that. My father was an alcoholic, too. And he would get ugly when he drank. And nobody was supposed to know that.

"Oh, oh," *maman* would say on Friday, "here comes another lost weekend." Dad would drink from sun-down on Friday to almost sun-up on Sunday. He would work all day Saturday and be drunk enough by sundown that he would start yelling at *maman*. He would stop his yelling early Sunday morning, go to sleep a couple of hours and let us sleep a few hours. He would then brush his teeth, wash, shave, comb his hair, put on his best suit and sit in the back pew during the earliest mass with the whole family. After church, dad would drink some more. Beer or whiskey. I always prayed he wouldn't drink wine.

Jacquie met me in the snow fort we had made. We recently had had a fight. This was one way of making up with her. I got lonely because there were no girls in the neighborhood. I had crossed the threshold where the boys didn't want to play as we used to. Not since Jacquie moved in and sissied things up. She would tease and taunt the boys to kiss her. Or to touch her.

"Lay down," Jerry would say to me thinking maybe I was Jacquie, "so I can lay down on top of you."

"Shut your face," I'd sneer. "You know what your mother would say if she knew what you just said to me."

"I don't care," he'd brag and saunter away. He knew he had made me feel dirty.

I wondered what was wrong with my old companion Jerry. Before Jacquie, he never demanded stupid things. Now, all of a sudden I was supposed to do what he said. My B-B gun shooting and Jim Bowie knife throwing friend wanted me to lay down? Humph. Get lost, creep.

Jacquie sat in the snow fort. With a muff. A fur muff. Something new daddy had bought her. I used to have a muff. When I was four, I thought. She looked babyish, and stupid, with a muff on when she was in fourth grade. South Grammar Elementary School. Where they taught the kids Spanish. In a Franco-American town. *Uno, dos, tres, cuatro, cinco, siés, siete, ocho, neuve, diez.* Jacquie insisted I learn Spanish. She crammed the numbers down my throat.

"I already knew how to count in French. See? *Un, deux, trois, quatre, cinq, set, sept, huit, neuf, dix.*"

"*Onze, douze, treize, quatorze, quinze, seize, dix-sept, dix-huit, dix-neuf.* See?"

"That's no good," Jacquie said. "Count in Spanish like me. More people speak Spanish than French."

"Where do they live?" I asked her. I didn't know any Spanish speaking people in town.

"Boston," she said.

"Boston?"

"Boston." she stated emphatically. "I'm going to live there someday."

"I live here. My *maman* speaks French to me and my dad, too. So, doesn't yours. Your daddy speaks French!" I argued. I figured if I hauled him into the argument for weight, she'd agree French was the better language to learn. My parents spoke French to me every day, but I was learning French at parochial school where the nuns taught us French. They would tell us the words we knew were not real French words and then they would let us loose to our parents so we could ridicule them as well. I didn't tell Jacquie this. I didn't tell her *"châssis"* was really *"fenêtre"* or that *"char"* was a word for *"l'auto."* No, sirree. I didn't tell Jacquie anything like that. I kept that one for another kind of argument. One with my dad.

"Ha, Ha, dad, *Mère du Bonne Conscience* said that your word for window is wrong, wrong, wrong, HA!"

"Tell *Mère* she's wrong," he'd growl back.

"Uh, uh, *Mère* said our French is a bad French," I sing-songed.

"*Mère* can go back to where she came from and ask them," he replied knowing full well what kind of French they spoke in Sanford and Biddeford, Maine. "*Ça pète plus haut que son trous c'monde là.*" End of argument. End of story. Still, I can see he was hurt. His pride was tripped-up. He was no longer as sure. Nicked. One more attack on the Frenchman from Water Street. And this time she had sprung from his loins. The errant daughter.

"You should speak French," he'd say to me.

"Not, me!" I would refuse.

"*Tu va l'regretter," i'me dit.*"

"No, no, not me," I would reply. Every time.

Uno, dos, tres...

Jacquie sat in the snow fort with her muff. I sat with my head bowed. My chest heaving with the happy news. I pictured my breasts which were not hernias after all. How do I say this? How do I break this wonderful news to my very dear, now, friend? The only other little girl in the world whom I could tell about my new breasts. I stutter. I stammer. She gets impatient with me. I tell her a substitute secret. "I knew that," she flaunts her superior knowledge. Hands in her muff. She fluffs it. My muff I remember had a doll's head on it. Hers doesn't I notice. Good thing I think to myself. Then it would look even more stupid.

"Hurry up," she says. "What did you want to tell me."

"I...er...I...started growing breasts." I finally let it out. The whole universe is stunned and hushed.

She stands up. Eyes livid. Speechless. Sneers at me and spits out, not quite caring, but caring too much:

"Is that all?" she hoots. "You called me out here so you could tell me you have breasts?" She turns on her heel and laughs at me over her shoulder, "I've had breasts for a much longer time than you! I even have a bra on!" Which she didn't, but she made her mother buy her a training bra soon after. We rarely spoke to each other again. Soon after that she moved. And then there were no girls who lived close to me.

The third span of our new bridge is all ready to be raised, but is delayed a little by operations on the second pier, which the contractor is anxious to have secured from a rise of water.

—*The Waterville Mail*, Vol. XXIV, No. 12, September 16, 1870

Chapter 10

Delayed a Little By Operations

Sears and Roebuck Catalogs were my sex manuals. All those women and men posing in their underwear. I would stare for hours at the bra and panty section. I was studying breasts. I wasn't shopping for bras, but for breast shapes. I was thinking of how I wanted my breasts to look. Some of those bras were so pointy they looked like they would kill you or the man that the woman would hug. Killer bras I called them. Bullet bras. Picked, pronounced pickid, bras. Pointy bras. And I tried to imagine the breasts that would go inside. And how they grew to such pickedness, rhymes with wickedness. Some arrows I used to shoot weren't that picked. Breasts were interesting. Men's shorts were, too, but I wasn't shopping for those kinds of bulges. Not yet, anyway. But I knew I wanted bullet breasts. I wanted to wear tight sweaters, too. Matching sets with the clips at the top and made of cashmere wool like the ones the girls on Mayflower Hill wore. Expensive sweaters that made you look cheap. "She's a sweater girl," *maman* would say. *Maman* would walk around in her slip ironing her clothes. My brother and I would chant and sing: "Sin woman, sin woman, sin woman."

"It's just my slip," she'd say, "walking around in the privacy of my home." And then sometimes she made us feel puritanical. Out of whack. Once when I was lying down in the bath tub, lounging, she walked in and then sharply told me to "cover myself up!" "A big girl like you."

"Knock, next time," I thought to myself. I felt no shame. She was wrong and I knew it. I had a right to lie down and lounge in my bath any time I felt like it. And I did.

And then I began to study real live girls for my breasts. I found one set I liked. They were on a girl in the eighth grade and I was in the fourth grade. I memorized her breasts so mine would grow just like hers. We were all in the TV room at school, a classroom with one small TV in it for 300 kids. The nuns would pack us in. Tight. To watch John Glenn fly off into space. I had a chance to stare at Marie-Pierre's breasts.

Boy, oh, boy. Those were good breasts. I wanted a pair just like hers. She even wore tight sweaters. Every chance I could I would look at her breasts. I would whisper to someone in the chair behind me just to get a good look at her breasts. I would be staring out the window and I'd slip my eyes sideways to get a look at those breasts. Once I found her staring at me because I was making her uncomfortable. To me, she had become Just Breasts. Then I realized maybe that I looked like I wanted more than just her breasts or something. But I didn't. I played nonchalant. Ate a few nails. Spit them out and told myself to take one last look. I knew she knew I was staring and it was becoming embarrassing to me because she started whispering to her friends and pointing to me. Breasts were on my mind then. She even wore a sweater clip. And pink cashmere. Her brother became a priest. With a sister with breasts like that? I could imagine having breasts like that.

And then, when I was 37 years old, they cut one of my breasts off.

Rum! Levi Lashus [*LaChance*], a Frenchman, who "keeps open quarters" in the old building next north of the Williams House, was investigated Wednesday morning by officer Edwards. Two packages or bottles of liquor were found—one in his boot and the other in a hole in the plastering. He was taken before Justice Drummond and fined $50 and costs. Lashus had just been legally warned out of the premises, on the supposition that he was selling liquor in violation of law—thus rendering the owner liable for heavy fine. Probably he will be expelled as soon as practicable, as the place has long been known as a bad one.

—*The Waterville Mail*, Vol. XXIV, No. 4, July 22, 1870

Chapter 11

One In His Boot And The Other In A Hole

The tiniest elements remind me of the longest days. My life now, so far away in time and space, cannot be easily explained by what is physically around me. But I have become who I have become because of all those tiny elements coming into place one at a time. I look at people in a crowd and I think how each one of them got here. Some woman somewhere took the time to be pregnant so that another human being could come to life. Nine months of hostessing. And then if the cards are played right, eighteen to twenty years, no—a lifetime of mothering with a few breaks in between if you get lucky or a baby-sitter comes along.

But a certain smell, a certain look or dish. A fly on the wall. Wall paper hangers and men on stilts swirling on a new ceiling with plaster after *mémère* had died. Her house was filthy and we were fixing it up to rent. Her sons, two of them, both alcoholics, one smart; and the other learning disabled, and reputed to be gay, sold their blood for beer money. The learning disabled one, he's kind of slow they told us kids, killed neighborhood cats for supper. Cats tastes just like rabbit they told me in reply to my disgust. What is he supposed to do? Starve? Cross-eyed, pigeon-toed, and a stutterer. *Mon oncle Pet. Mon oncle Pet-Pet* for short. Fart-Fart we used to call him behind his back. We didn't think it was a name that was bad. It was more a sound to go with the character of the man. One of the unfortunate ones. The neighborhood was full of them, so he wasn't that outstanding as far as characters go. Besides, he was just my uncle. A member of the family. We used to roll his and uncle Clem's cigarettes on Sunday afternoons when *mémère* was still alive and the whole family would get together to drink beer, talk, smoke cigarettes and lament, as *maman* would say.

"*Les moudgits lamenteux.*" *maman* would say. "*Moudgits lâche. Ça sait pas faire rien. Et ses sœurs la même moudgits chose. Lamenteuses.*"

"I can't," she'd mimic wincingly. But then they would bring her new wool in the fall and it was *maman* who would sew my two cousins new winter coats. For awhile. Till *maman* put her foot down.

"They can sew their own goddamned coats," she said. Dad had really treated her bad that weekend. She wasn't about to eat his shit and theirs, too. "I am the smart one," she'd exclaim to his calling her *"moudgits dâsse"* all week-end. "Yeah, you're the stupid one," I would say under my breath to him echoing her.

Theirs was a double marriage in the families. An older sister of dad's and an older brother of *maman*'s had married earlier on. Family slung gossip said about the older couple that the husband was a drunk and the wife was reputed to be lazy. Depending from which family you were slinging the slander. The feud between the two families was well established long before *maman* and dad were married. So when dad brought *maman* home to meet his *maman* and *papa*, she was not well-received. My father said too often to my mother that he married her out of revenge. So that she could pay for what her brother had done to his sister. That, in his more drunken moments, was his claim to why he married my mother. When he was sober he was more penitent and sorrowful as to what he had said and done. Come Monday morning before he went to the mill, it was her turn to talk. The woman was angry. And she slammed his lunch into his lunch basket for him to take to the mill and she crashed the cover down on his thermos full of coffee she had funneled in and she gave him a piece of her mind. "If you think…" They'd load up the cannon and start all over again come Friday night.

When we lived on the farm in Detroit, Maine *mon oncle Pet-Pet* came to help us on the chicken farm. He would be too drunk, blind from his crossed-eyes or *gauche* because, after he had been in the barn, we'd find dead chicks—the ones he had stepped on. The work was too complicated for him.

But he was good at making us laugh. We could act silly with him.

"Say *'penut, penut, penut'* tree times widout laughing," he challenges us. Spitting and laughing, wiping his mouth free of backwash from the beer with the back of his shirt sleeve. He takes another a swig of beer. He has buck teeth, too. And he has a lisp. He is a clown with no need for a mask or makeup.

Dad didn't like us laughing at him.

"Say it! Quick. *Vite! 'penut, penut, penut!'* he giggled.

So we would try.

"Penut, penut…"

He sat, with his eyes bugged, his fly unzipped, holding his Schlitz by the neck, silently mouthing the words along with us.

My brother would crack up!

"I can't, *mon oncle*, I can't do it!" my brother would give up after three or four tries.

My turn. I would try.

"Penut…"

"ha…ha…h…ha…" *mon oncle Pet* would snigger.

"*Mon oncle*, don't make me laugh."

"OK, OK."

"*Penut…*"

"ha…ha…ha…ha…"

"*MON ONCLE!*"

"OK, OK. I won't laugh," he'd say.

"*Penut…penut…*"

"ha…ha…ha…ha…"

"*Mon oncle*, you said you wouldn't laugh!"

"Did I? I won't laugh dis time. Just say it—tree times: '*penut, penut, penut.*' I bet you can't do it"

"Oh, yes, I can. See. '*penut, penut, ha, ha, penut.*'

"Doesn't count," he said "because you laughed."

"No, I didn't."

"Yes, you did. I heard you laugh." "See," he said, "you say '*penut, penut, penut*' tree times widout laughing."

"Let me try again!"

"OK. Dis is the last time."

"*Penut, penut, penut,*" he says tree times. "No laughing." "*Ris, pas!*"

I turn my back to him. "*Penut, penut, penut!*"

"*T'as besoin de me garder, là!* See, I told you you couldn't do it."

"*Penut, penut, penut!*" he crowed. And took another swig of beer.

When the first French-speaking immigrants appeared in Waterville, this 'Plains' section of the town was a vast, thickly wooded area with a few tiny clearings here and there for grazing. The whole section up to what is commonly known as the 'flat', was a sort of peninsula, surrounded on the East side by the Kennebec River and on the West by a narrow, marshy stream having its source at the further end of Pine Grove Cemetery. This muddy brook slowly curved along today's King Street and emptied into the Kennebec Canal around the bottom of today's Sherwin Hill…

...Others found similar work in Waterville in the 1830's and 1840's. Some robust French Canadians were hired during that period to clear an extensive wooded area which was to become, in 1851, the Pine Grove Cemetery.

—*Albert Fecteau, Master's Thesis, 1951*
The French Canadian Community of Waterville, Maine

Chapter 12

The Pine Grove Cemetery

All the vegetation around us has a way of knowing our secrets. The trees droop their leaves spying on our lives. The grasses bend their blades to catch our sounds. And then they gossip about what we have been up to lately. They know the past of whoever has been around. You can feel it in their eerie silence as they stand there or as you walk by. Whenever I face west, I face the setting sun, Garden of Eden's hidden gates and eavesdropping, chattering trees. Spreading rumor. Tattling. The trees and grasses know. It is their mystique. Their power. When I face west and I imagine I am seeing Garden of Eden, even as a child, I am seeing the gates to the Tree of Life. The trees are angels in disguise. The trees imitate Garden of Eden's special opening, and the younger you are the more magic you are, so you can see more of the underworld—the secret world all around us.

As a child I am in awe of the make believe because of the reality it carries. The possibility of chance. One of my walking home from school fantasies was that when I get home from school there will be a tractor trailer truck full of toys I won in a contest. I never entered my name, but someone did enter my name for me.

You hear about Charlie Verrow who dresses up in his Superman costume and jumps off the roof of the garage and breaks his arm and nose. Everyone wonders what got into that kid's head. Too much TV they say. I sit there wondering— what went wrong? He should have been able to make the leap. I shake my head like everyone else, copying them, but inside I think to myself, I bet I could do it.

What? Jump down all thirteen stairs in one jump and land on my feet at age four? Of course. I can do it. I do it all the time when I get tired of going down the stairs the regular way.

A hand reached out and grabbed us from that grave, I tell my friends years after the event happened.

I'm sure the man in a long duster raking leaves in the cemetery looked just like Michael the Archangel. He was standing guard, making sure we wouldn't get into Garden of Eden. After one of our raids, I saw him framed by an apocalyptic sky when he stood at the top of the hill, pointing at us with one arm to mark us as doomed. We locked ourselves in the shed, my brother, me and Jerry-Ron-and Ricky. Just in case.

Do the angels on the granite pedestals at the entrance of the cemetery blowing their horns, covered with gold leaf, come to life at the end of the world? I bet they do. I can almost hear them announcing the end of the world today. Every time we drove by on our way to Belgrade and Great Pond, my brother would point out the angels.

"Those angels are going to come alive at the end of the world," he says. We are sitting in the back seat of the Rambler.

I'm forty-one turning into the driveway to the Catholic side of the cemetery to go see my parents who are buried there and my brother who gave me those end of the world predictions for the angels coming back to life and I think about what he told me. I hope he's right.

My brother died when he was forty-one. You never think you are going to make it past the age of the person who died that you feel close to. He and I were always in the cemetery—playing. It was our playground when we were kids. To come see him buried here is one way of being magic. Our ghosts linger around the headstones. They keep burying new people here, but back then, when we were kids, we kept track of the new, fresh graves. Like we were the inspectors. Grave inspectors. Children loose in the graveyards—Protestant and Catholic—a fence divided those who were going to heaven and the eternally damned. To a Catholic, to be buried on the Protestant side was the same as going to hell and doomed. No questions asked. Here was hell and here was heaven. Garden of Eden was at the bottom of the hill. Before you got to hell. Which was the Protestant side of the dead.

People would say to *maman*, "How can you live next to all those dead people?"

"It's not the dead that bother you," *maman* would say to shut them up.

In the woods, on the hill, playing as children, we came upon two graves: one was marked "Mother," and the other was marked, "Baby." The two markers, solitary in the brush, stopped us dead in our tracks. We ran home to tell dad and *maman*. They both knew the graves were there. The old cemetery had been on the side of the hill, he told us, and they decided to move the graves to the top of the hill. For some reason the city did not bother to take the mother and child. Why? How did she die? Was it in childbirth? No, I don't think so, *maman* said, because they would bury the baby with the mother then. Was she French like us? No, because the gravestone is old and it would have been written in French. Where did she come from? Probably somewhere in Waterville. Maybe she was a poor person, *maman* told me. Poor people were buried by the city in a pauper's graveyard. That was a city plot once. She probably was too poor to be buried anywhere else. Do you think there is a father buried somewhere near them? Maybe she had the child all by herself. Back then, that would have been a shameful thing to do. I don't know about her, you ask so many questions, talking machine. *Maman* was done talking about the woman and baby in the woods.

I went to visit the lone graves by myself. They were hard to find in the thick woods. Separated from the rest of the dead as if they were shunned in death as I imagined the mother and child had been shunned in life. I made up a life for the woman and her child in my mind. I clothed her. I gave her a house. I designed clothes for her baby. I let her live. I stood by them to talk and stare at the headstones as if they would talk back and then I sat on the baby's headstone because it was small when I got tired of standing and talking to them. I would tell them everything was going to be O.K. I knew she was there. I knew she was dead. I knew she was all alone. I would not forget the Mother and Baby. No one remembered who she was. It didn't matter.

My grave plot is beside my brother's—my long-ago cemetery playmate.

As children we walk the roads in the cemetery. The place seems endless and far away from home. We drag sticks behind us. We have a special way of walking when we are in the cemetery. One for all seasons. In summer, we lope and drag sticks behind us leaving a trail like Hansel and Gretel to find our way back home. In fall, we pile the leaves and jump off the top of the hill down its slope. In winter, if you step lightly on the snow, you don't break through. Only the headstones are visible. We sit on the wrought iron lawn furniture in the winter breeze. Spring makes the whole road system muddy and the sap runs in the trees. We go every night to collect the sap from the line of maples running up the hill. There is a brook nearby. We have a meeting tree at the top of the hill. Every day at a certain time we meet there with the other neighborhood kids to decide who we have to scare first. Each other or the cemetery men. They are the workers who have parched brown skin, are silent like ghouls, smoke, and wear dusters. They scare us more than we know. But one of our favorite games is to try to sneak up on them, headstone-to-headstone, six or seven kids all at once and scream, ahhhh! at the cemetery men to see if we can get them to chase us. That's when we head for the shed.

So my brother is buried in our playground. The children playing with the dead. I like the bravery of the deed now. Back then, it was just a place for us to play. Ask the trees, they can tell you all about us.

The migration of these sturdy French Canadian immigrants, often known as *'Canucks'* was very puzzling and sometimes annoying to some native citizens. Each year their number increased and the line of Yankees retreated...In the early days there was bitter feeling between the young men of the 'Plains' and the young men of the town...the struggle...stemmed from personal animosity and hatred...by the end of the 19th century, they had reached a point where their presence merited consideration.

—*Albert Fecteau, Master's Thesis, 1951*

Chapter 13

Canucks

Spirits walk past us and leave their scent. It is the only way that the formerly alive can communicate with us—by leaving a smell behind. Or a blast of cool air. Like swimming in a spring-fed lake, every now and then you swim through a cool spot. Lying awake last night in my bed I smell something. It was a little unpleasant, but not entirely. Some spice. Crank shaft grease. Sawdust. Fish scales. Hot chili peppers. All mixed into one. Lying awake, unable to sleep all night, I knew my father was nearby.

Today is his birthday, I think to myself. If he were alive. Born at the turn of the century, his sensibilities were of a 19th century man. He was lost in the 20th century. I think he had lost his bearings when his father and grandfather entered the mill to work. *Pépère* worked at the Hollingsworth and Whitney and then tended his inner-city farm. My father was the good son who helped his *papa*, as he called him, with the farm animals, raising vegetables, and selling the produce to local people. They had corn on the cob for sale by July 4th. During the Depression they sold it to the rich people at a dollar a dozen. *Pépère* wore garters on his sleeves when he worked. He was a farmer by heart; a mill worker by fate. Too many mouths to feed in *Québec*. So *pépère's papa* walked from Canada to the U.S. and worked on farms to make his way. He came to Waterville. Married a local woman and settled in to the routine of turning a farmer into a city slicker.

Waterville, a township on the Maine map, is not a large land mass, but it is heady on its own fumes because of the "Ivy League" school which makes its home there—Colby College. The workplace for many Franco-Americans as cooks, janitors, secretaries and maids. Zamboni drivers. Toilet bowl cleaners. Salad preparers. Rarely, do Franco-American children attend Colby College. Although children of workers can attend for free. Few choose to stoop to that level of social climbing. Who would they talk to when they came back from the foreign land, and while there, who would understand them? The French body language is all different than what is bodily believed in at the Ivy League school. The gestures of being brought up French does not prepare a child to compete in the world of high finance, Jaguars, the smell of money emanating from the leather of the shoes and lying down in bed with creamy-skinned, silken-haired silver spun women. Or, men. So Colby is safely tucked away from the onslaught of the French who took up residence in Waterville to work in the mills. The women of my neighborhood were the playthings of the Colby men. "The girls on Water Street" were girls the Colby men were told to avoid. They might get the crabs. I am one of those women who the Colby men were told to avoid on a Saturday night. Their spirits stank when they walked in our neighborhood. It was the rotting shoe leather.

Pépère gambled. He gambled in the backroom of *Druoin's Café* with other men. During the Depression he amassed a sum of $10,000. Five card stud. As his granddaughter, with a lust for poker, I know how he won. By instinct. He didn't play poker thinking; he played by heart—the same way he grew his corn. To win. By feeling the power of the cards speak to him. I know because I could do this till my father jinxed my game. My father insisted I think when I played poker. Watch which cards have been thrown he insisted.

"That's not how I play," I tell my father.

"How do you play poker?" he demands to know.

"I feel the cards."

"What do you mean 'you feel the cards'?" he is puzzled.

"I sense what is in my hand and what everyone else has in their hands. I play for aces. I play for face cards. I feel the power of the cards. I know who has what and I play my cards by what they say to me."

My father makes a face at me, disregards what I just told him, and directs me to play by thinking.

"I can't play poker that way," I tell dad.

"How else can you play, then?" he is skeptical.

"I know what I know and I know what the next card played will be and I feel my way through the game," I tell him. I feel my confidence slipping. I feel my magic way of playing cards seep out of me. I am ten years old trying to explain to my father that I play poker the way I bet his *papa* played poker. By instinct. By feel of the cards. I can almost hear the deck vibrate on the table. I am not clairvoyant, but I know where the Ace of Spades is and who has the king of spades to beat my queen by the shape of the fan of cards in their hands. I win. My husband plays his hand—straight flush. I lay mine down—royal straight flush. This time we are playing poker in the kitchen in my *pépère's* house. I smell his spirit as he walks away from me—compost, sandy loam, sulfur from the mill, a fresh pack of cards, old money rubbed by many, and choke cherry wine. My legacy is to play poker. I inherited it from my *pépère* who died with enough money accumulated from playing poker to support his family two years on steak every day for lunch after he died. That was his claim to fame. Corn on the cob for sale by the 4th of July and poker playing to win.

FIRE!! FIRE!! FIRE!!

Insure with Boothby
—*The Waterville Mail, Vol. XXIV, No. 17, October 21, 1870*

Chapter 14

FIRE!!

I wonder what we have to do with some of the people who wander across our lives? Jacquie was one of those people. She was a skinny, bony-kneed little girl with brown eyes, country songs on her lips, cowboy boots, and a Bonnie and Clyde in her heart. We often compared our approaches to getting boyfriends. I preferred my Wild Bill Cody approach to being a girlfriend to her machine gun brand of friendship. I could be tough, but I had a heart. Mostly, I did rope tricks. When the boys in the school yard, who were kept to their side of life according to the crack in the cement walk leading to the church, planned an ambush to get a girl's jump rope, my jump rope was never confiscated. I was ready. Two days in a row, my boyfriend from across the room, three rows of seats away, sitting with the dumber boys, as we were sat according to intelligence, made his plans. All of our grades for the quarter were tallied and totaled, divided to get an average of all our grades combined and was used against us. Our own quarter grades—be they good or bad—were used to seat us by the average's score. I often wound up sitting in the last seat of the first row so I could conduct a constant surveillance of the room. One way of survival in the parochial school system was to possess information which could come in handy. Sitting in the back gives me the luxury of spying without turning around. Besides, in order to use the dictionary, I didn't have to even get out of my chair. It was on a podium just behind me. I could look words up without getting up. My boyfriend's grades did not match his face. He was a cute boy, but dumb according to his seat number. Sixteenth or seventeenth out of twenty boys. I was a constant, sixth out of twenty-four girls. Except once, I got the first chair. One time I was the smartest in the class, but that was much later.

He was going to steal my jump rope. I could see him making plans with his friends from my spy chair. I thought of a master plan. Wild Bill Cody would rope him. Or, yelp, hippy-ky-yay and lasso the devil. He looked just like a hellion this boyfriend. Black hair, black like a crow's turning blue in the sunlight with purple glistening and blue eyes. Freckles. White, white skin. An embarrassment which never faded. Laughing as a cover-up. Valentine sender. One Valentine in my box in third grade was from a boy. One boy sends me a Valentine and he turns out to be a devil. Chinese lanterns on the Valentine and his name signed in the back. "Be mine," the Valentine says. I carry it home like it is a secret. Someone finds it in the house. One of my brothers. They find out where this devil of a boy lives. Every time we drive by they tell me that is his house. I stare out the window and say, "I have no idea who you are talking about. I don't know any boy by that name." I am lying, because I lie to keep me safe from their teasing. I stare at the house and will him to show his cute face. It is summer vacation and I'm in love. Third grade and I'm planning our wedding. What will we name our children I think. I have to wait till after high school for us to be married. This is going to take awhile I can see. I make plans in my head for my wedding dress. The reception. Our house. He is trying to get his friends to help him steal my jump rope at lunch.

My father made me this jump rope. He makes me a jump rope every spring. He brings a piece of rope home from the mill in the bottom of his lunch basket. He steals this rope and then hides it beneath the dish cloth kept in the basket with all his dirty dishes. When the shift change happens at the mill, *maman* and me wait in the hill to go get our man. We put on his coffee before we leave and time it for three minutes once it starts to boil, turn it off when the coffee is cooked, then we jump in the Rambler, cross over the Kennebec River to Winslow to go get our man at the Scott Paper Co. We are parked in the hill with all the other mill worker's wives. *Maman* waves to Bertha. *Ma tante Marie-Claire* is not here today. Her husband, *Lucien*, is working a different shift.

All the women wait for their man to walk out, show the watchman/ guard the inside of their *paniers*, lunch baskets like picnic baskets, and then she drives down the hill to get her man. Dad brings out my jump rope every spring. He gets home, takes off his shoes and socks, fills a pail with water and Epsom salt, gets the black electrical tape out of the tool drawer he keeps in *maman*'s kitchen, some scissors, soaks his feet while sitting in his rocking chair because he's been walking on concrete all day at the mill and he says: *"J'ai mal aux jambes."* For the hundredth time, he measures me against the rope because every year I have grown and I need a longer jump rope. He cuts it off at a good length with his pocket knife he keeps on him and then he winds the ends of my jump rope with black electrical tape so it won't unravel. He does this for me every spring.

"*'tChan, bebite,*" he says, "Here is your new jump rope."

I have been sitting at the kitchen table patiently watching him wind the tape. I know better than to ask him when is it going to be done. He would only tell me what he always told me when he was doing something and I asked questions

"Watch," he'd say, "and you will learn. Don't ask so many questions. Watch, and learn by watching. You'll learn better that way. If I tell you, you will learn nothing. *Bâdre moé pas. Tanne moé pas. 'Gard', bin, p'tite pie.*"

So I watch.

And he winds and winds the tape around till it is thick enough to create a ridge so my hand won't slip when I am skipping rope. I wait.

"Take it," he says, "don't lose it." That means, I'm not making you another one.

I take the rope and I go outside to jump. I am not as good a jumper as some of the other girls. I am shy and I don't like to be watched. I like to jump rope alone. I know all the rhymes. I scream them at the top of my lungs as I jump. Me, with my French accent. Everyone speaks to me in French; I answer them in English. English salt and peppered with French accents.

First I whisper: "Rhea and Stephen sitting in a tree, then I yell: k-i-s-s-i-n-g/ first comes love/then comes marriage/then comes Rhea wid a baby carriage."

The devil boy is in the corner whispering and pointing. It is almost recess time. I don't want to lose my rope which my father stole and made for me. He may not make me another. My rope does not come from the store with wooden handles like the other girls and it is not just plain rope, mine is a black and yellow plastic interwoven rope which is heavy and makes a loud satisfying snap when it hits the pavement. The devil boy cannot win. I have my plan. Me and my Wild Bill Cody plan.

I am in the alley beside the school, jumping rope and I feel a rush of wind, and a loud yell from devil boy and his friends. I am ready for his show of love. The bigger surprise is the louder yell which comes out of shy me as I begin to twirl my heavy plastic rope as if it were a lasso. Hey-Ha! I scream cowpoke style as if I were home with my brothers. I am going to rope this boy! Hey!-Ha! Devil boy comes too close. I snap him in the cheek and raise a welt on his face. I can see he is in pain. I keep twirling the rope Wild Bill Cody style. I am high on my power. The boys slink back to their side of the sidewalk crack. I am still swinging the rope in the air. The other girls who had been playing all around me have cleared out as well. I am there alone, triumphant, swinging my heavy, plastic rope above my head, yelling, yelling, Hey-Ha! Hey-Ha! Hey-Ha! Everyone says: "Get out of her way! Get out of her way! Let me out of here! She's crazy! She's gone nuts! Help!

I didn't lose my jump rope, but devil boy never sent me any more Valentines. either.

A very good and enjoyable (we know) public temperance meeting was held in the Universalist Chapel at West Waterville, on Thursday evening. It closed a session of the Templars. Half a dozen fluent and pungent speeches, aimed at different points, kept the audience well entertained up to the time of an early adjournment. By call from the chair, Joshua Nye, Esq., always a favorite speaker in an earnest temperance audience, led in a varied talk, in which the progress of the cause, with its present political bearings and suggestions, was presented in his usual frankness.

—*The Waterville Mail, Vol. XXIV, No. 10, September 2, 1870*

Chapter 15

Fluent and Pungent

Last night I went to hear that famous woman writer from Northern Maine with the French last name and claims she's Scotch/Irish. She takes after her *maman*. Like we all do. *Maman*s are important people. Especially to middle-aged orphans such as myself.

I try to think what about me is French. I am confused and I try to pin-point it. It must be the way I cook. *Maman* always starts her spaghetti by frying salt pork which she leaves to cool and I eat as an after school snack. Fried salt pork rinds. They are my favorite. Deeply browned and crisped. Very salty. I drink tons of water after I eat the fried salt pork. I consider this a delicacy and a very special treat.

My husband and I are in *Québec*—we go to *l'Ile d'Orléans* to search out the ancestors. *Jean Côté*, the one who came across from *Mortagne-au-Perche* in the 1600s is buried there. Along with others. We stop at a restaurant to eat. I see that fried salt pork is on the menu as an appetizer. I go wild. I order some. The waitress is skeptical about my authenticity—like I am not a real princess and I won't feel the pea—or eat the salt pork fried up and served in a bowl. I lick the platter clean. She has to go back to the kitchen to save face. I take two pieces of the fried salt port with us back to the hotel room to share with my son. He won't even look at the stuff. Another day, I fry some up at home and he eats it like the good, little French boy he is. Getting right in line for a heart attack, too. But for a taste—fried salt pork can be a real treat. *Lard sallé* I call it. In Canada, they are called *Oreilles de crisse*. Sounds like Christ's ears to me. Eating fried salt pork in memory of the temple guard who got his ear sliced off by one of Christ's men. It's like the living Bible.

Salt pork is everywhere. Fresh string beans in the pressure cooker with salt pork thrown *in pour donner d'bon goût*. Salt pork in the beans. In the soup. *Soupe aux pois*. Salt pork as a staple. No French-Canadian, later called, Franco-American, cook would be caught without the salt pork in her kitchen.

Dad told me how he made his salt pork when he kept pigs. In the cellar, crocks, full of brine and pork sides. Weighted down with a wooden cover to keep the fat from floating to the top. "Why?" I wonder out loud. Sometimes I was an embarrassment to my father by how much of his knowledge I was ignorant of and had no idea I was supposed to have ingested what he knew through the process of being an offshoot of his sperm and my *maman*'s egg.

Growl.

He would growl at me when I didn't know what I was supposed to know. Growl.

I stand there, guilty.

"Because, *bebite*, fat floats," he said.

"Oh."

"Why wouldn't the pork go bad?" I ask.

"Because of the brine," he said "and the root cellar was always cool."

I am a skeptic. "Root cellar?" "Cool?"

"T'sais comment ça faisait tout le temps frais dans l'cave?" i'me d'mande.

"Yes," je lui réponds.

"Bin, c'était comme ça. The root cellar was always cool."

"You mean you kept food from spoiling down cellar at *mémère*'s house?"

"Bin, oui!" he said emphatically.

"Cool." I'm impressed. I think about the root cellar.

I remember the sandy loam in the floor when I used to go down the narrow steps as a child. The light switch at the top of the stairs was an old-fashioned ceramic-twist-of-the-switch. It was very dark and dank. There were two parts to the basement. One where the furnace was, where the wood was stored and another behind the wide planked wall with a door which led to where the earthen floor kept things cool. The root cellar. To go along with *mémère*'s summer kitchen.

Dad gives me the recipe for the brine. Like I was going to need it soon.

I make a note of the ingredients and method in a general way, but I forget the quantities. Salt, sugar, saltpeter. Water. Glass crocks. And cool storage. O.K. The meat and the salt are layered and then brined.

I cook with salt pork.

I am freshly married. I buy some pork ribs at the grocery store. The meat when cooked gives off some kind of smell which I have never smelt. Surrounded by food all my life and I never took an interest in its properties. Except that it be set before me on the table and I ate it. Now that I'm in charge of the oven's hell gate, I'm a good gatekeeper. What was that smell?

I complained to *maman* and dad about this smell coming off the ribs. It was so strong we threw the meat away and boiled some hot dogs. We ate out on the porch. I almost got sick.

Dad said: "They waited too long to castrate the pig before they slaughtered it."

"No…" said the skeptic. I think: boy he's really lost it this time. Castration and cooking?

"Yes," he is insistent and sure of what he is saying.

"*Maman*, dad says the pork tasted funny because of the pig's balls. Is that true?"

"Oh, yes," she emphasizes the yes to make it sound like "Yeeees." "He ought to know," she says "he slaughtered pigs with his father all the time. And when we were first married. Your father used to keep pigs right where we built the house."

"Pigs are buried all around here," he says.

"*Écoute moé*, if they don't castrate the pig at just the right time, the juice goes all through the meat and makes the meat taste bitter. It would not of hurt you to eat that meat. It tasted funny, that's all."

"It stank!" I protested loudly. "I gagged on the smell."

Then he tells me the proper way to slaughter a pig.

"I had a special mallet," he said, "and I would hit that pig right between the eyes to knock the sonofabitch over." He points to the middle of his own forehead with the middle finger of his left hand. He sits in his chair, leaning back, handling the armrests nervously. His hands never stop.

"Keel right over. With one good blow to the head." He says this and I know it is true. My father was a small man, but he had the strength of a man twice his size. Maybe three men.

"We would string that pig up by his feet with a block and tackle after we had fattened him up nice on corn and slit the troat. I would cut the troat right in the big vein in the neck and drain the blood into a big *chardron* to make some nice blood sausage. *Mon Djieu! c'est assez bon, ça.*" He is not even talking to me anymore, he is in waking REM.

"I had cut the balls off the boy pig and so my pork meat never had that bitter taste you tasted," he is proud. A good farmer. I sit and wrinkle my nose and the sight pig killing must made. He wants me to know my way around the farm yard. Just in case. Or to give me what he knows. You never know when there will be another Depression.

"Then we would butcher the pig," he explains. "Some nice hams, chops, bacon, and all kinds of good stuff. Out of the head we would make *creton* and then pickled pig's feet."

"Everything but the squeal," he laughs.

"Boy, oh, boy, those pigs knew when it was time to die. They would be so noisy, running around!"

I'm not sure what to think. I can't forget how to make salt pork or how to slaughter a pig. I have all this information and no place to put it. I am *Canuck*, I live in Maine and I cook with salt pork. Dad used to make the salt pork and hams and chops and bacon. I am a cultural dead-end. What am I supposed to do with the lessons he gave me? Who am I supposed to tell the ways of his people? How does his lessons fit in with the way I live?

After *maman* died I took him to the grocery store—this former pig farmer in his spare time when he wasn't working his doubles and triples at the pulp mill—and I was going to show him my fool-proof method of choosing a good cut of meat, always tender in the meat case. I showed him the way that the grain of the meat ran and then how some were so tough you couldn't sink your finger into the muscle. Dad does not get the trick. He slams his thumb down into the meat, instantly breaking through the plastic.

"Boy, you can really tell which piece is tender doing it that way," I say dryly.

"What did I do wrong?" he asks.

"Do it like this," I say, demonstrating restraint.

"Push very softly down on the meat and don't slam your thumb down so hard."

His next try is much better.

"Now," I tell him, "you will never bring home a tough piece of meat again!"

It is his turn to be skeptical.

"First, you choose your price and how much you want to pay."

He was headed toward the 'best cuts' because they were more expensive.

"Money does not mean a more tender piece of meat," I state.

He looks at me with his New York Sirloin in hand.

"Put it back," I tell him. "and come here."

"This one, dad, feels just like butter. See? You can sink your finger into it and it doesn't feel like a tough piece of shoe leather at all. This is the one you want."

"*Ça coûte pas cher,*" i' me dit.

"Price is not how you tell a good piece of meat." I will not be moved from my superior place of knowing.

I tell him how I discovered this method of choosing tender meat. When I was seven or eight years old grocery shopping with *maman*, she would take forever to choose her meat. I would lay my arm on the glass case and then lay my head my arm and slide along testing all the meats for softness. The redness of the meat looks beautiful and luscious to me. I cannot stop looking at the beauty of the red cow meat. I am enthralled by how good the meat looks. Raw. I could eat it on the spot. I stare and I sense a blood lust in me. I am mesmerized by the look of all the rawness. I lay my head on the case and I stare at the meat. The meat in the butcher's case at Ted's corner market is even better looking. I see *Armand's* blood stained apron and his hands which he wipes on it. I take my time walking by the meat case. I walk slow. I stare and I lean. *Maman* goes on to do her shopping, but I stay with the meat and I touch its softness. Rejecting the toughness. She tells me, "Don't touch the meat." or "Don't break the plastic." I touch the meat. I break the plastic. All along the meat case are finger prints and holes in the plastic where I have gone along and touched and touched and touched.

It was reasonable to suppose that the death of the young man in the lock-up, last week would suggest to the proper authorities the propriety of taking immediate measures to put that filthy place in condition for uses for which it is designed...It was not only unsafe on account of fire—as the death of young *Roderick* has proved...most of the persons thrust in there are drunk...and once before a man...kicked over the stove and set the straw on fire. Now there is no stove or other means of fire; and it was inhuman to put a drunken man in such a place, to lie from Saturday till Monday. "But what else can I do?" was the reply of officer Edwards.

—*The Waterville Mail, Vol. XXIV, No. 20, November 11, 1870*

Chapter 16

Other Means of Fire

Being born last in a family is like walking into a movie that has already begun. The action has been going on for quite some time and you walk into the theater where everything is dark, everyone else is sitting and eating their popcorn, candy or drinking their sodas, you have to find a seat for yourself and find a way to catch up to what the story is about. You have to understand the main plot, the clues, the theme, tempo, musical score, heroes, stars, action shots, caution: danger, mud puddles of happiness, saloons' backroom games, beauty parlors, dance halls, feel out the other hombres so you won't get your face smashed in too hard or get pounded out for not knowing the plot well enough. And, since you were born late in the show, the plot thickens. It is a lot like being caught in a gun fight at sunset and you forgot to bring your guns.

Family life will do things to you. Harm you. Scar you. Scare you. Salvage you. Contain you. Confine you. Define you. There you are waving into the camera. Smiling. Waving. Avoiding the lens of the old-fashioned movie camera after a few minutes because the light is so bright that you are blinded. It's a moving camera and everyone just stands there. *Maman* and dad went out to buy one of those cameras in the sixties. Everyone we knew had had one since the fifties, but we got ours in the sixties. Three minutes of film. Silent. Except for the noise of the projector. Life moves at a clip like an old Charlie Chaplin film. Everyone moves faster in the home movies than they ever did in real life. There I am at age thirteen, the gift table hostess at the Silver Anniversary Party. Dad had to be released from Utterback Hospital. He was suffering from depression. He could have gone to the state hospital for nervous breakdowns, but he wanted to go to a private hospital. They were giving him shock treatments. He asked *maman* who that little girl was with her when she and I went to visit him.

"*Ouéyons don', Ray, c'est ta fille,*" mamam said, shocked.

"*Ma fille?*" he looks terrible. Pale. Drawn. Unshaven. Lost. What the hell were they doing to my father in this hospital? They were supposed to be helping him. He couldn't even remember me. He tells us he is forgetting many things. Whole blocks of his life are gone from memory. Wiped out. Years later he still says that he cannot recall certain times of his life because of the shock treatments.

The waiting room at the hospital is dark and dingy. Shades drawn to keep the view out. The outside world is a non-entity. We cannot go see him in his room, but we must wait for him to be brought to us in the visitor's room. They bring him in and I am happy to see him. Until he says to *maman* pointing to me: "Who is she?"

I know what it is like to be forgotten, but not remembered is worse.

I was thirteen and he came home for the Silver Anniversary party. He kisses her. He looks like a killer. He hates the party and all those people. He is happy to get away at the end of the day. To go back to the hospital. Away from all those people and the noise. For years afterwards, I polish the silver they received at the party. Some of it is real silver and it takes me a long time to polish the crevices. I think of the home movie of the party—I wish he would have shaved closer. He always had a five o'clock shadow.

Sojourner Truth, the famous old colored woman, gave her testimony in Providence the other day against the women she saw on the stage at the Women's Suffrage Convention the other day, I thought what kind of reformers be you, with goose wings on your head as if you were going to fly, and dressed in such ridiculous fashion, talking about reform and women's rights? 'Pears to me you had better reform yourselves first.

—The Waterville Mail, Vol. XXIV, No. 20, November 11, 1870

Chapter 17

'Pears To Me

Where I come from is where I want to be. I used to want to come from somewhere else. I pretend myself in some other context. More white. I am a Franco-American girl growing up in a French-Canadian neighborhood. *Un p'tit Canada*. Rumor has it that we give out sex for free. Like candy. We have a reputation of being uninhibited. We have body language, but what we Franco-American girls are saying isn't what the Colby boys and *"les anglais"* are hearing. Things get confused. The Colby guys take a ride down our street to pick up some women. Not so they can fall in love and marry them and things like that. We side-step them on the sidewalk. Things are less formal in the sixties, but the scent of superiority coming off Mayflower Hill is still the same. All things flow toward the river in those days before waste treatment plants—so down on Water Street we had twice the amount to deal with—our own and the stuff flowing down in attitudes from up on the Hill.

Body language is an art. Body language is a code. Body language is a secret. Take leaning for example. French women lean. They lean on lamp posts when they talk to the guys. Leaning is sex standing up, but leaning is a casualness of posture, too. I lean because I am tired. Women who lean are inviting with their bodies to do some other kinds of leaning. We French girls can lean and not mean what the leaning says. Dad or *maman* would kill them. Repression goes a long way in a strict, Catholic neighborhood. There is leaning because you are tired and there's leaning-with-intent toward someone else. I was leaned toward by a priest once. A priest leaning against a post at a dance despite his tight, white collar stuck in his breast pocket, looking like a toughie dressed in black. The collar resembles a tongue depressor sticking out of his pocket. Something suggestive or subliminal. "Poor devils," *maman* says about the priests. She knows they lack leaning in their lives. She understood their loneliness. Despite her unhappiness in her marriage, she felt their sacrifice was much more sorrowful. "That's no kind of life," she says. "Always alone." Same thing for the nuns. Whenever I come home and tell her I think I want to be a nun, *maman* would say: "Oh, my God. Have they been brainwashing you again? Do you want to be lonely all your life? That's no way to live." "Get outa of here…you don't want to be a nun." I go back to parochial school and be silent whenever the nuns start to tell us about their lives of wonderful sacrifice. Don't we hear the Call? The Call? Don't we know in our hearts Jesus wants us to be just like them? Holy and good. I sit there silent and feeling like a traitor, but I know what *maman* will say if I tell her I want to be a nun.

"You don't know what you want," she said. "Those people never had a life. They go into the convent when they are very young, never went out on a date, never kissed a man, never can leave the convent. Their mother's funeral passes right in front of the convent and they cannot even go to the church. Get outa of here. Don't tell me you want to be a nun."

So I sit when they talk about being a nun. I put on a very-interested-in-what-you-are-saying face and pray that they shut up pretty soon. I nod appropriately, like the fake I am. The other girls, the teacher's pets, the first, second and third chair girls, sometimes the fourth chair girl, too, all say they will be nuns. I sit in the back and say nothing. I am asked. "Are you thinking of being a nun?" they ask, diplomats for chairs-in-the-front and teacher's pets anonymous. "I'm thinking," I tell them.

Maman, at least, has someone to fight with and then, there were the times when things were O.K. between her and dad. Like when they work on their flowers together. Or their lawns. The place where I come from, *chez-nous*, looks like a park. People would walk down the street from their hot, third floor apartments with their babies to let them run around on our lawn and around the pond dad had dug and piped water to from the stream in the woods running off the cemetery. It was their place of calm. And beauty. How ironic. All I want to do is run away from there and get myself another identity. I want to be a white girl. A girl from Mayflower Hill. A girl with an English name. An English identity. An English sexuality. An English sensibility. An English everything. Instead, I have French as French could be. I want straight legs and not the bulgy kind I was born with. I hate my legs. They embarrass me. Curvy. Big calves. Like baby cows on a girl. Everyone laughs at me when I tell them. *Maman*, too. They hoot. "You'll find out…" they sing-song. "What!" I wonder, mourning my funny looking legs.

And the feet, the feet have got to go. Peasant feet, that's what these things are. Feet that have walked barefoot in the garden for centuries. Bunions from ages past. A whole history of a people written on these ugly, ugly feet. I look at *maman* and dad's feet and I see that my chances for pretty feet are not so good. Hers are just as ugly as his, but for some reason I blame him for my feet.

"Gee, thanks, dad, for the ugliest feet in the world," I say to him. "Look at your ugly feet!" I exclaim, wailing. "How did they get so bad?" I want to know the whole story of his mutilation and in it may be a clue as to why my feet are so bad looking as well. Some kind of foot binding torture on our side of the world?

"I wore bad shoes," he says. "Inexpensive shoes."

What kind of shoes would deform feet to that extent? Consequently, I have good shoes bought for me at the most expensive store in town. I can only wear sneakers in the summer. No support. Ruin your feet. How can you ruin already ruined feet? In gym, or Girl Scout Camp I see English-speaking girls with pretty feet. Straight toes. No bunions. I am on a campaign to straighten out my feet. I walk barefoot all summer to straighten out my toes. I concentrate on one foot. I am only fifteen. My bones are still soft from my baby life which is not too, too far away because I have fresh memory of being two still, so I can straighten out my toes. The pointed shoe era is still here. It's the sixties. Woodstock is next summer. I will hear about it on the radio and wonder how can so many people hear about a concert and show up. I am barely aware of it while it is happening. My feet take up all my attention. I want pretty, English-speaking girl feet. Not French-speaking girl peasant feet.

Julia *Paradis*, a French woman, wife of Frederick *Paradis*, was found dead on the road between Bangor and Oldtown on Tuesday. She was a woman somewhat addicted to the use of strong drink, and though the affair seemed enveloped in mystery, the verdict of the jury, after hearing evidence, was, that she came to her death from exposure to the storm or from cause unknown.

—*The Waterville Mail, Vol. XXV, No. 20, March 24, 1871*

Chapter 18

On The Road Between

I get the idea of going away from my French beginnings when I do go away from them. I move to a farm in Detroit, Maine. I go to the four-room school house and there are boys in the classroom all the way to the eighth grade. Cute boys. English speaking boys. Some with French last names and some with German last names, but they are all farm boys here. Or live next to farms.

Dad wants a farm. He is trying to get better. Dealing with his depression. His *maman* dying the year before adds to his confusion. This is the time just before the shock treatments. For years, every Sunday, on *prenait une ride sur les terres*. We go for rides on the farm. We are looking to buy a farm. Dad is a farmer by heart. Or by memory. French people eat dirt. He can tell what a soil needs by touch. A little lime. A little potash. A little more fertilizer. *Un p'tit peu d'ça*. We all pile into the car and go for rides on the farm. Sydney. Oakland. Winslow. Albion. The Forks. Benton. Clinton. Burnham. Vassalboro. Augusta. Finally, Detroit.

Whoever left France in our ancestry in the 1600s, left with the idea that they were going to get themselves a farm. A collective memory. On to *Québec* and its stubborn, rock-ridden earthen crust.

Still moving, coming south to New England. French-speakers loose in a place of discontent. To work in the mills. To keep from starving. To earn a living and then to go back to the farms in *Québec* and a way of being which is French. Sort of. Someone lost the map of France. In my family. *Mémère*, *maman*'s *maman*, used to say she thought some of our people came from France. We all spoke French. Someone lost the history book or never wrote one either. Me, I was just plain leaving the whole thing behind me and I was going to be an *Améritchaine* girl. Marry me some *améritchain.* Live in a big white house. Be perfect. No curls in my hair. No leaning allowed. Except I do lean, because I forget. My butt sticks out when I lean. I am vaguely aware of my posture and what it says. Sometime I want my body saying what I cannot say with my mouth. One boy gets what I say.

I want body language gone, kaput. Get rid of all that junk. My French accent is the first to go. The kids in Detroit, some strawberry blond, pink-faced, freckled girl made fun of my "mudder," "faddur," "choo cherity tree Water Street," so I pretend I am from Boston. My brother is gone to college there. I practice when we bring him. Crash course in accents. I listen to Bostonians and I imitate.

Kid power. I learn overnight. I make it up. Shut-up, yer egnoraaant. I drink tonic instead of sodee.

Losing oneself is hard to do. Hard work. Remaking a girl into another girl is tough work. Being white, and *Améritchaine*, not French, Franco-American, is snob work. I become a snob. I ditched my father because his threes will always be trees. *Maman* is not so low class. Her threes are threes. She dresses nice when she goes uptown. *On monte au fort,* we always say. Going up to the fort for supplies. Like I'd been doing it for centuries. Except this is the 1950s and 60s. I walk away from myself. I'm on a road not to self-discovery, but to forgetfulness. Drop all that French stuff and pick up a squeaky, clean fake front of English tea cup society on the highway to hell bound for nowhere. My neighborhood gives me away. To some, I am cheap trash no matter what I do. I am a "Water Street Girl and you know what they are like…" Even the Summer Street French boys say that. They live one tier up from the river, no actually two. The first tier is no longer inhabited. The second tier on this small town five layer cake is Water Street, the next ridge of the ancient riverbed is Summer Street, on par with the same ridge that the cemetery sits on and then you have Silver St. and Main St. level where you continue to climb onto where the air is thin and rare until you hit the Cool St. ridge before you reach Mayflower and Colby Hill. Mount Merici and Cherry Hill Drive are up there too. The French have infiltrated all the levels in this town. Depending on how much upward mobility your family was into.

Nobody fucks on Mayflower Hill. Not their daughters, anyway. Or so the legend goes. Only Water Street girls fuck. And give crabs. That's what Water Street girls are like. The Chez Paris. Local bar, sometimes a grill and a strip joint. Therefore, we all bump and grind. Ethnic women, debased by sight.

The men who go to Colby are warned to bring condoms when they visit our neighborhood. To visit the nurse's office if anything funny shows up on their skin. Pricks. Some Lolitas, looking for love, give in or out depending on your beliefs, do get recycled. My brothers have this thing about French Virgins. They need a personal sacrifice for the sin of our being French. So I am not approached. Not by Colby guys, anyway. It is their illusion of sanctification. My sexuality is a discussed topic. "Côté! Go get your sister!" "You go near my sister, you baaastard, and I'll kill you," my brother tells him calmly. They know how he feels. So I am unapproached by the neighborhood guys, too. I feel as if someone sprayed an extra can of Raid when I walk on the sidewalk. The guys clear a path. I am high on my power until I find out why they let me pass.

Although I am approached by your garden variety of sex offender on any given day. There is some kind of other way of being in operation here. I am warned about the strange men. Depending which season it is, I have my pick to fend off. Something about expressing sexuality is very different in this neighborhood. Some old men, leech. Other old men in the neighborhood don't leech and are fixtures, characters of a time long-spent in these parts. *Souris.* The Candy Man. *Danse-pour-moé.* It is the only name we know him by and what he does. It is a request. As children we play with him. He loves to dance. We know this. We appreciate his pleasure. We hide in the bushes and yell out our request, *"Danse pour moé!"* He stops on the sidewalk, dead drunk, with music playing in his head and dances a dance of light-footed joy. Like a bar of music measures out a routine. He stops and walks a few feet until we call out again. *"Danse pour moé!"* He dances and dances moving sporadically up the street. We play with him. We watch his dance in fascination. I wish I could move like that. So some men wouldn't harm us at all. Those we know.

We know the others, too. The ones who do more than just lean. They do fuck. Or, aspire to fucking. Leer. This is urban—small time stuff, but the men lurk just the same. A beat up, always down on their luck kind of man. Operating on their own rules. Not allowed to play in the Mayflower game. Not even worthy of scrubbing the toilets on Colby Hill. Or, like *m'tante* Annie, amused by the sexual antics of "those college kids." Disgusted by *les moudgits tchuls, m'tante* Annie, hot after a day's work, says, "oh some of those girls are sweethearts, call me *maman* and treat me nice, but some of those rigs, well, I wouldn't want my girl up there with some of those boys. *Les moudgits faces."* Married by age sixteen, one of the oldest of *mémère's* seventeen, *m'tante* Annie has very little patience with those spoiled brats—except she understands their youthfulness, the one she never had. "You are married a long time," she always forewarned. Keep away she meant. Take your time to get married. I didn't. I married soon after my eighteenth birthday to another eighteen year old whose mother had to sign for him so he could get married. "Take your time. You are married for life."

I sit in the classroom with the nuns. They talk Jesus. Joseph. Mary. Heaven. Hell. Holy Communion. The Baltimore Catechism. They talk sacrifice as a way of life where your reward will be great in heaven. Snort. *Maman* always insulted God when she was mad at him about her life's situation. She sing-songed, sarcastic, whining: "Your reward will be great in heaven...how about a little reward down here, Jesus! Jesus. Jesus. Jesus. *La moudgits vie."* From the convent, I walk home. Depending on what the season is, I am side-swiped sexually. Visual confrontations. If I knew then what I know now, I could have told the men, containing myself: "Your gaze is hitting the side of my face." Then, well, then all I said were very highly crafted insults and looks that could kill. I practice before the mirror. Snort. Sneer, snarl. Sniff. Slowly look sideways at the crawling vermin and say with some effort at stooping to their level, drawling under my breath

some remark of supreme disgust. One of my personal favorites is: "Drop dead."
Long on the "o" sound for effect. Curt, too. Certainly, disrespectful of the old
men. The really old men. Like the thirty or forty year olds. There was no one
around to protect me so I taught myself a way of killing without touching. They
would crawl back into the holes from which they had come. We had our daily
routines. They stole from me visually, at age twelve or thirteen, and I sharpened
my verbal claws on their hides. I was quite ignorant of the sex act in reality, I
could only sense their hands on me in places I would not take kindly to being
touched. It would call for a swift kick to you-know-where or a bite, sink my
teeth in, dirty fighting my brother would chide, any place I could get a hold onto
and spit in the face, a real clammer in the eye. Two spits maybe. I go through
this tunnel of leering doms, dirty old men, every day at 3:00 o'clock. It would
happen in the spring, two brothers, woods cutters who came down from *Québec*
and who would stop watching TV long enough to come up onto the street to
watch me walk by. My eyes narrow to a slit and I literally spit at them. They
laugh and go back downstairs to their basement apartment. I am so good at what
I do that after one season of my dirty looks in return, only one brother persists
in coming to the street level to view me. The other is shamed into reality. *"T'as
pas honte, toé?"* He has no shame. I would swear, too. Under my breath. *"Moudgits,
Crisse de Tabadnac."* Goddamned, christly tabernacle. Guess I told him. Tomorrow
the nuns will tell me how I am a temple of God and I should keep myself pure.
Maybe the nuns haven't been to the temple lately. Have they seen how many
people go to the temple? Can I borrow your habit so I can walk home, *chère?*
Here, let me pinch your cheek till the skin comes off in my hand like you always
do, too, *Mère de Bonne Conscience.*

Management of Brooms—If brooms are wet in boiling suds once a week they will become very tough, will not cut the carpet, last much longer, and always sweep like a new broom. A very dusty carpet maybe cleansed by setting a pail of cold water out by the door, wet the broom in it, knock it to get off all the drops, sweep a yard or so, then wash the broom as before and sweep again, being careful to shake all the drops off the broom and not sweep far at a time.

—*The Waterville Mail, Vol. XXV, No. 19, November 4, 1870*

Chapter 19

Far At A Time

There are some thoughts you can entertain for days because they are like candy to the brain. Sweet, sweet thoughts. Resting easy on your mind, you lie in them for the sheer pleasure of their silkiness. Soft and flowing thought patterns; brain waves in undulation across the sea of synapse. And then someone slams a door or comes into the room asking where the cat's flea powder is or can you help me find the can opener (it's hanging under the cupboard) because I want to cook. Cook is opening a can of ravioli. I'm impressed. Gourmet cooking is macaroni and cheese that comes in a box. *Maman* is rolling over several times in her grave. I sit and stitch the quilted coats in echo of the land. I think of all the quilts I've seen and I recognize these quilts in the earth's patterns while in flight from Bangor, Maine to Lafayette, Louisiana. I'm going to see a friend and look at some roots or something like roots in Louisiana. I've been to Canada and France, now I'm going to see the Diaspora in Louisiana. There are *Côtés* everywhere.

"It's like a treasure hunt for you?" my airline seatmate inquires. Earlier he looked at me and remarked: "You don't look like no coonass." I'm looking at him, "What's a coonass?" His treasure hunt remark was a way of saving face.

"Coonass?" I am puzzled. I can just about guess what he is saying though.

"You know," he says.

I shake my head no.

"That's what they call the Frenchies down in Louisiana. Coonasses." he informs me. I am not amused. He can tell. So he switches to the buried treasure routine.

"Yes," I smile to myself. A treasure hunt. How can I miss when looking for buried culture? I can't. How does he, as a perfect stranger, as only strangers can be perfect, know or feel the need and the joy of exploring deeper depths of the self. A few questions from him; statements, explanations from me and he instinctually knows the importance of my sojourn to Louisiana.

In Memphis, four small children run to meet their mother—screaming, happy, one yells, "new shoes!" They are all over her. "Bright, shiny, new shoes," he yells. Kids know their mother's lives like a well-traveled land of their own. I am thinking of my own children, who used to be small, and when I was their port of call. It is one of the silky thoughts I keep with me, even though some days I felt like a stevedore.

I forgot that we crossed another time zone. I thought I was going to miss my connecting flight. I had a chance to live 2:30 all over again. We flew south and now we are turning right. *Mon Djieu!* The land below is exquisite! I wish I were a quilt artist. The land is so beautiful I would copy its patterns in quilt. And then I think, I have already. Unknowingly. It is from 10,000 feet in the air and the vantage point of flight that I recognize that I have echoed the patterns of the earth in cloth and quilt. And so haven't all the other quilters—all the other women who piece cloth in response to the land on which they live. How can we have come to the conclusion of cloth repeating the patterns of the earth? How can the women of bygone eras, without the aid of flight know how far-reaching their quilt patterns vibrated in tune to the patchwork of the earth? Or is this one of those times when everybody knew but me?

"There's power in those quilts," a friend once said to me. "Why do you suppose everyone wants to have one or to get their hands on the family quilts?" I stand there wide-eyed, rooted, remembering. Caskets and quilts.

In flight, I write a poem in honor of the quilt:

The View From Flight 5410—Northwest—Memphis-to-Lafayette

What is a quilt?
A quilt is a woman's garden
fields of cloth
echoing the earth
harrowing—plowing
seeding
weeding
reaping
repeating
the gifts
  first fruits
forests
groves
crazy quilt fluvial plains
snaking rivers.
geological fossils
road bed
farm labor

cain raising cain
swirling sweeping
river bed
bound to the river
to the oceans
to the sea.
raised threads
borders between
field & forests
crazy quilt
ordered pattern
a cloud's shadow
belongs.
shadings
gradations
"in search of our
mother's gardens"
grown
in cloth
quilting
earth-bound
echoing
repeating
the meter, measure
of the land—
pull the clouds
from the sky
cotton batting
fluff
  stuffed

―――――――

Quilt
earth &
    sky
unite.

―――――――

"There's power in those quilts," she warned me. I simply nodded yes.

Excursions.——...The Lightfoot Base Ball Club, of West Waterville accompanied the first excursion and played a friendly game with the Katahdins of Dexter, beating them in a score of 33 to 30.

—*The Waterville Mail, Vol. XXV, No. 8, August 19, 1870*

Chapter 20

Excursions

I lost the threads of the dream. I dropped the stitches of a whole evening's work. In my lap. Like I was only fooling around and dreaming all night long without meaning a single thing that went on in my mind. The world of the upside down, the prides of clouds casting their shadows onto us creating shade. Dreams cast similar shadows as clouds creating shade. Like memory which is really manifestation of who we are today. The accumulation of lived lives playing itself out daily in gesture, remark and habit. The original blue print or intent lost through the years. How old is that habit of mine when I stand there in a stance which screams out my *maman* and her habits. Familial postures. Expressions of origins like a map telling us where we came from and where we are going. Each one an accomplice of our fingerprints.

We inhale our dead. Or we ingest their manners. I am sitting eating my supper with one elbow on the table. "You sit at the table just like your father did," my husband calmly remarks. "Why do you do that?" he asks, curious. I've had a highball. I sneeze every time I drink just like dad did.

"I know I am doing that," I reply, "I'm not sure why I do it." It is a habit I acquired after he died. Is this my way of being with my father? To become him in posture. I am acting out an obligation or a privilege. It feels like both. I study my aunts' hands waving or coming to rest as a bird in flight while she talks or sits there. I am doing research on body language of the family women. Who am I when my body speaks? With certain aspects of the body language lost in me I feel like a modern fraud. Like there is a fashion in body motions such as there is in popular dance. Franco-American women in their families and communities have signature gestures that signals silent speech. Certain things mean certain things. I understand the language well, but I don't always speak it. Movable body parts speech coming off ethnics scares the pants off the non-participating other ethnics—in Maine, the body speakers would be the Franco-Americans, French-Canadians, or French heritage types and the non-body speakers would be the non-French heritage types. "Me," I say tapping my own chest with the right hand's middle finger, "me," repeating for emphasis both the word and the motion, "I am a French heritage type." *Canuck*. I sometimes get my signals confused.

In a Laundromat in France I watched with grave interest three people, a man and two women, talk about some renovations they were planning together about the laundromat. Three large people stood in a three-foot square floor space, faces pressed close, yelling, gesticulating, arms flailing, hands waving, pointing, tapping chest, palm splaying and retreating, only to begin this commonplace-in-France drama of intense conversational exchanges all over again. No one was angry. Just passionate. Intense. Body languaging. Telling story their way. I am no stranger to this kind of conversation and I am looking for Mr./Mrs./Ms. Good Body Language everywhere. After a century or two of being suppressed, whenever I hear someone speaking with an original body accent, I want to pin a medal of bravery on their chest. Prejudice is a good teacher of conformity. If that is your goal in life.

We had moved to Detroit, Maine in search of my father's collective memory of *"sur les terres."* He was looking for the "Good Farm." I attended the four-room village school. My brother told me, "you are going to *Die* in *Die*troit." The locals pronounced the place: DEEtroit. While making fun of their pronunciation, he meant the place was boring; what really happened was worse than being bored.

"You talk with your hands," Sue in the pink-checkered dress, strawberry-blond tells me at age eleven.

"Oh, yeah? What did I just say?" I quip.

"You must be French," she accuses.

"You must be a genius," I sneer. I had told them all at this school I was French. Maybe this wasn't such a good idea I am finding out. Considering her loose reputation she has gathered for herself by age eleven, if we put child prostitution and being French on the same level of social outcasts, and often that is the case, I didn't think she, the slut, not being French herself, but free with her new tits with the farm boys, had much to crow about. I was going to tell her how cheap she was giving away her breasts for free, but I thought of how deep this would hit and hurt so I swallow my words and glare out the window. I am hurt by her remarks about my being French. She doesn't stop there, miss-can-I-sit-on-your-lap-so-you-can-feel-me-up. She laughs at how I pronounce my words. How I speak. She repeats the sounds I make. Sing-song. Counter-sneering. Screwing up her face.

"You don't want to keep your face looking like that too long," I tell her, "it may be permanent."

My next insult has to do with body odor. I got this one from my big brother. I'm not quite sure I know its exact meaning, but I say it anyway.

"Do you always smell that way?" I remark, "Or don't you ever wash?"

"Thoo-turty-tree Water Street," she replies. "Turdy, turdy, turdy, turd." In other words, I'm shit.

"Your mudder and your fadder," she crows. I stand there muted. For the first time in my life, I hear how I sound to other people because my first language was French. I am eleven years old.

"You're just jealous because I can speak French and you can't." This was my last attempt. This insult comes from my *maman* telling me how the other boys would laugh at my brothers pushing me around the neighborhood in Waterville in the baby carriage. They would just laugh back and say to the boys, "You're just jealous because you don't have a baby sister to push around in the baby carriage." So I was a Madame Queen in a Carriage viewing my kingdom just as my daughter was a generation later in Deering Oaks Park . Sue was just jealous. That's it. She was jealous, but it wasn't because of my accent. I figured it out why she was jealous later on. Some boy liked me and not her. The most popular boy. The cutest boy. The sexiest boy. The most daring boy. The most blue-eyed, crow-black haired boy.

Sue hooted. "Of being a dumb Frenchman? HA!" She walks away in her pink gingham checkered dress which was too tight with her so-called famous breast the size of walnuts. Her too-tight perm, cut too short flying on her head. After that, I stayed in the classroom all winter during all recesses to read. I read sixty books that winter which I bought with my allowance I earned working in the chicken barn. Almost the complete set of *Nancy Drew* mysteries. *Trixie Belden*. *Donna Parker*. Mysteries are my favorites. And I read all the bookmobile books I could lay my hands on. I hardly open my mouth to speak. I'm working on a new accent in secret. A Boston accent. I'm practicing Bostonian speech patterns in my girl brain and come spring I no longer say "thoo-turty-tree" or "mudder and fadder". I enunciate and pronounce my words as if I had chewed them forty times each. I lived at Two-Thirty-Three Water Street with my Mother and Father. Very tea cup. Except we never use saucers when we drink coffee or tea *chez-nous*. And, cool. I have new insults which I picked up while in Boston. "Shut up, yer ignorant," or "Hey! Hey! Not interested," or when someone was being a pest—"You want to call off your dogs?" I used these special insults for years. Even today. Sometimes someone will ask me: "Do you come from Boston?" I just shudder and laugh to myself. Should I send myself a sympathy card for dying in Dietroit or what?

WANTED

At the Mail Office a girl to set type. One living in the village preferred.
—*The Waterville Mail, Vol. XXV, No. 17, October 21, 1870*

Chapter 21
WANTED A Girl

We all married our high school sweethearts. There was no opportunity for opportunity. Falling in love was highly regulated by certain rules of courtship. Each family has variations, but the rules are similar. Sexual experimentation did not necessarily mean penetration into the forays of love or the family unless there was an engagement ring to it. Virginity was a high commodity in our neighborhood—usually going to the highest bidder which does not mean possessing worldly goods. Bidding meant having the balls to visit the girl at her home. To break into the family code. Fathers are deep, dark shadows to walk across to get to their daughters. When the father wasn't on a binge.

I married young. Everyone I knew married young and usually their first serious love. Adolescent lovers taking a walk down the magic carpet ride in the middle aisle in the Catholic church. Middle aisles are hard to find if the church is round. But we find it just the same and we walk toward future happiness and dreams before decomposition. We married young because that was the fashion. Hope chests, dish patterns, stainless steel pots and pans, bakeware, and silky nighties. Playing at a role which we see all around us. Only guessing at ourselves and creating a whole aura to rival the greeting cards' well wishing. We are serious in love. A love which we pledge forever. It's a long way from romance to reality, but we travel the road. Some of us die young from cancer. Too many. We have children and some of us divorce. Experience love as adults. Which is more tart than as children.

I dance with him at the "Y." He has a hard-on. When we waltz he presses himself near me. In my innocence, I think that his hard-on is a permanent way for his penis to be. I wonder where he puts it walking around in his too-tight jeans. We sit on the floor in the darkened gym for break between the song sets. We make out. Heavy kissing. More hard-on. We do this for weeks. All through the winter. I always leave the dance with a stomach ache from being kissed so much. I go home and write the nuances of his touch on me in my diary. When I want to remember the lovemaking on the floor between dances I take out the diary and read it to revive the sensation of his kiss and shared breathing. My father is reading my diary, also. His mother was a snoop, too. *Fouilleuse.* Always sneaking and reading other people's mail. One night when he gets drunk and does his yelling thing into the wee hours, he begins to quote my diary. Screaming at me and telling me how cheap I am. *Maman*, not having read my diary because she believed in privacy and practiced it, says, "What is he talking about?" Usually he is screaming at her about her looseness which is a fiction in his mind. All women are whores according to him. His sisters had illegitimate children when such a thing was still a shame. I listen to him for a few more minutes making up my mind as to which is the bigger crime—me kissing my boyfriend or my father reading my diary. I decide dad is the bigger sinner and that I have a right to kissing. "He's read my diary," I hiss at *maman*. She is shocked. She reels back. She cannot believe how filthy minded he is. "What a filthy pig," she states. It is a known fact to her how far he will to depravity. He may have got this far, but he won't get any further with me. I will just hide it so well that he won't ever find it. That's all. I get smarter and more suspicious of him. In all things. I don't stop kissing. With my whole self involved. We kiss for hours on end. Two or three hours at a time. I don't think I could stand anyone in my face for that length of time now, but our kissing was only second to breathing and sometimes we just did that together.

"How sweet," someone told me yesterday about my love affair with my husband of twenty-three years.

"How cute," said another. They are a lesbian and a woman who just told the four of us sitting there that both she and her husband had had previous long-term relationships. Those kinds of love are above sweet and cute. There I sit, and Annette as well, with our marriages made out of sweet and cute, being judged as immature or not having quite lived, yet, because our love affairs were not of the daring kinds which involves lesbianism or break-ups and divorces and re-marryings.

I contend with my supposed non-experienced life lived out as a married virgin, I tell myself in my more skeptical moods. I'm not so sure that they are wrong in their sweet and cute evaluations of how I fell in love and discovered sex. We were married a year before he realized that I was orgasmic as well. He assumed I was his outlet. I was a budding feminist, but sex was not on the agenda as of yet. In our first apartment, after one year of marriage, one Sunday afternoon we dropped onto the king-sized bed which we had bought the summer before our senior year in high school, and made love. Sort of. I was as usual disappointed and I became very angry and told him of his selfish ways. If he couldn't do any better than that, he could kiss my ass. He was shocked. "What do you mean?" He was truly puzzled. No one had told him girls were able to come. I had taught him what he thus far knew about sex because no one had told him anything. A couple of years back I had to tell him where babies came from. We are nineteen years old the two of us and we are already like two old trees side-by-side with our roots intertwined. This occurred to me years later, that to sever our ties, would be to kill the root system of the two. Extricating myself from him would be like cutting my own roots.

"You are not finished with me," I scream in a whisper.

"What?" he is dumbfounded and very, very hurt in his face. Ashamed. He is sorry.

"This must be awful for you," he says. He thinks a few more minutes, sitting on the bed's edge and his head hung down. "You must feel used," he states. It will be the trademark of his understanding for the rest of our married days. Once he understands, he understands. His insights are deep. He is often silent, but he still sees even if he doesn't speak it out loud.

"All this time," he says "and you never said anything to me. Why?"

I sit there, in my own inexperience, and sigh. "I don't know." I was willing to put myself away. To let my own desires die. To not admit to my own sexuality at the expense of my ignorances. I was a school girl going to convent sponsored dances with him when we began dating, this is when the Catholic Church began it own journey into adolescence in the 60s, and we would kiss and press our bodies close on our way to hell against the brick building until the priest would come out to get us. I had no shame. I was not aware of how I looked. I was only feeling. I'd kiss him in the back of the armory leaving the dance for a few minutes. The cop would shine his light on us and tell us to move on. I'd make a face at the cop's back and stay to kiss him one more time in defiance. We would park at Colby Pond and dishevel all our clothes, untuck, unzip, unsnap, unhook—one-handed—we got good at it. Until the "fuzz" came and told us to move on. Steamy windows, parking lights on, and he would say to the police, O.K. just like he wasn't weak from the heat of our passions.

After I told him about my disappointment of him not taking the time to bring me to orgasm, it never happened again. He became a tempered lover.

A group of women are driving to Bar Harbor. It is 1988. Talking about orgasm. One is a widow. She tells us about her lover. He goes on business trip and meets her when he can. He has had several women in his life. He is an old rival of her dead husband. A former partner and friend as well. They were always entertaining back and forth. His wife subscribes to hysteria; he fucks around. He's taken up with my friend, to alleviate her loneliness. She, after over twenty-five years of marriage, and the birth of her three children, discovers she is orgasmic. She is shocked! Pleased. Gloating. I'm appalled. I ask the question: "Didn't you, didn't you ever masturbate when you were a girl?"

"I was never aware of my own body," she replies. This is a very intelligent woman. She never gave herself permission to explore who she was.

I do not say what I am thinking. He husband strutted. He would hitch his pants and strut. Older than she, he was so cock-sure of his prowess and here she is telling us, that she has had her first! orgasm with her lover. Her husband was a shit. She is so happy and we say better late than never.

"I was so stupid," she chastises herself. I tell her about my first year of marriage and my anger at my husband about his stupidity. She is amazed. That young and I knew what I wanted or I could state my needs. I cannot imagine living with a man and not telling him off for his selfishness. But then again, I have seen stranger things.

Another friend was married four or five years when she discovered one time during their love-making that she was orgasmic.

"Oh! Oh! What is that?" she yells. She and her husband tell me and my husband this story one night as we are playing cards in our Portland apartment.

"I didn't know what was happening to me!" she exclaims.

"Stop, stop," she said she said. "No, go, go. Move. Oh! Oh!"

"She went crazy," he interjects.

"We did it again and again right after that one time," she tells us very serious "I wanted to feel that one more time!"

"We didn't come downstairs all afternoon!" he crows.

"The people we were staying with got tired of hearing me yell!" she laughs.

"Someone came in and heard us and asked the people what was going on," he relates.

"Oh, Connie has just learned to have an orgasm and they won't stop doing it," they explain.

That's all I ever heard about women and their orgasm except in the magazines.

Maman used to measure how close and how real the kissers would get in the old movies.

"They are not really kissing," she'd say if she felt the actors were faking it. I was five, six, ten. It looked like their lips were pressed together to me.

"They're not really kissing," she would judge. If she knew some movie stars were having an affair, or had an affair, she'd say, "That Carole Lombard stole Clark Gable from his wife. What a slut. Look at her, she is really kissing him and they are not even married. You can tell that they are in love. He is kissing her right on the lips. They are really kissing." At the time of the making of *Cleopatra*, with Elizabeth Taylor and Richard Burton, *maman* would talk about them as if they were in the neighborhood. "That bitch," she'd say "she can't make up her mind about which man she wants." She went to see the movie just the same.

"And that Katherine Hepburn, her and Spencer Tracy were together for so many years and they weren't even married. He had a wife. They just loved each other." For her it was that simple. Then she would bring the Catholic Church into it.

"They won't even recognize a man who is divorced," she complained. "The couple cannot even get married in the church." That was a major drawback in life for her.

Thinking of her own lumpy marriage, she would say, "I can't blame anyone for going after happiness." I wonder how much she really believed that.

"Now, Paul Newman," *maman* would announce to all of us. "He could leave his shoes under her bed anytime." Dad would just sit there, silent, as if she had never spoken or give her one of his sideways looks with those eyes of his. "Your father is such a hypocrite," she'd counteract.

The bridge is progressing finely, and under favorable prospects. The fourth and last span is nearly ready to raise, and will be in its place early in the coming week. The stone work on the piers is nearly out of danger from an ordinary freshet, and extra crew of workmen provided for next week will speedily make all things safe...Those who hope to use the bridge for their winter business are not likely to be disappointed, though the old ferry boat will doubtless be kept in readiness for western travel.

—The Waterville Mail, Vol. XXV, No. 13, September 23, 1870

Chapter 22

An Ordinary Freshet

Zayre's Department Store. We are a team. Me and Bunny. Bunny is her name because her mother named her that. She was almost born on Easter. Bunny is my best friend. We are high school juniors. We work in the store for those two years of high school. Bunny comes from a poorer family. More kids. Her father works at jobs which don't pay much and her mother does not work at jobs outside of the house at all because there are just too many damn kids. Bunny has to work if she wants to look fashionable. She gives most of her paycheck to her mother. To help with the up-keep of the family. This is 1970 and 1971. Her mother has picked out her future husband. Bunny is raring to go with life, not marriage. She is confused.

She saunters over to the service desk. She and I are Customer Service Representatives. CSRs. We are the night shift. I have two jobs. I go to school in the morning till noon, and then as a work practicum, I go to Public Finance to work as a bill collector. I call people in Swans Island, Bath, Belfast who have borrowed money from the finance company because no bank would loan them money. Poor people. Destitute. Down on their luck permanently. I feel like a spoiled brat with my comparative luxuries calling to ask when they think they will be making their next payment. I sit with my pile of payment cards before me and dial the phone. Sometimes the people are nice and tell me when they will be sending their next five, ten or twenty dollars, depending on how much they have borrowed. These are the delinquent accounts. Some of the borrowers pay the money back without the call to remind them their payment is due. I work with Dena, another high school business secretarial student. She types envelopes. Fifty to sixty envelopes at a sitting. I had started typing envelopes too, but they needed a bill collector, so I got the job. Dena is too shy. I am shy, but I am bold, too. We work with Joy, office manager, to- cute-a- a-button woman from Winslow. The man in the drugstore next door comes in to seduce her every day. He gets a cup of coffee from the back and sits down to shoot the breeze. First with Joy and then with Mr. *Poirier*. He always flirts with Joy.

"Why don't you and me go sit in the back room, Joy, and we'll talk about the next thing that comes up," he laughs. He is semi-serious in his flirt. Goading. Crying out for help.

She is upset. Laughs, not quite pleased. Slams her balance books around. Clacks the keys on the calculator that could serve as a lawn tractor if you found a way to attach a blade and some wheels it is so large. He can tell he went too far.

"I'll be seeing you," he goes back to selling toothpaste, hemorrhoid medicine, rubber bands and chewing gum.

I come in one afternoon and Joy is bubbling over with gossip.

"He left his wife!" she exclaims.

"Who?" I am puzzled. Mr. *Poirier* is sitting at his desk so it can't be him.

"He just up and left town and his wife and kids!" she is triumphant. Gloating. Pleased and puzzled. How could he be such a dummy is written all over her face. And her face replies, of course, because he is such a dummy.

"I'm not surprised," I remark. The guy was a loner. Gaunt. Thin. Not much there to offer and not much to think about. I can see him doing that. Who would marry a guy like that I think. Scary.

I pick up my cards to begin calling. Mr. *Poirier* is in a mood to chat and philosophize. We never get any work done when he starts talking. One hour passes. Two hours go by. Sometimes, three. I call two people and go to my second job.

Maman comes to get me so I can go home to eat some of her delicious food. Pork chops and mashed potatoes. Chicken pie. Spaghetti soup. Veal cutlets. Steak. Chicken and peas. *Tourtière*. Salmon pie. *Creton*. Hash. "Rabbit hash," dad calls it. Meatloaf with bacon strips on top. Salted spare ribs. On her lazy nights, scrabbled eggs and mashed potatoes. She is a good cook. I like to eat her food. She drives me to Zayre. I work six to nine. She will be back to pick me up in three hours.

Bunny is walking toward me where I stand behind the service desk. We process refunds and exchanges. Run hourly checks on the cash registers out front. Make announcements for lost children. Call for the departments for price checks. Do lay-a-ways—new ones and take payments. Cash and with the new way to buy things—credit cards. I can see by the way she is walking that she is angry.

"Why didn't you tell me!?" she hisses.

I check to see if the public announcement system is off.

"What?" I ask, bewildered.

"Do you know about douching?" she demands to know.

"Yes…" I hesitate. I can see where this conversation is going and I wonder if it is my responsibility to tell Bunny about douching. We have gone double parking, she and I, with the boyfriends, soon to be husbands. Mutual groanings and car shaking. It can be a little embarrassing knowing someone else's moves like that. Something you'd never let your mother see you doing. Bunny and her guy sit in the back and we sit in the front to park and neck. It's my boyfriend's car. Once we went to the drive-in to park. They got out and took a blanket out on the grass.

"Why didn't you tell me about douching?" she is very upset.

"I thought you knew," is my lame response at the moment. I'm not exactly thinking on my feet having been shocked by her request.

"I feel so stupid," she wails.

"Why?" I am curious what brought this on.

"They were talking about it in the breakroom, Mrs. *Raoul* and the others, even her son, who was a former boyfriend of Bunny's, "joking about it, and I didn't know what they were talking about." She is humiliated. "They laughed at me."

"Did they explain what it was?" I ask cautiously.

"Yes," she replies miserably "but I felt so stupid. I'm going to be a married woman and I don't know anything! My mother hasn't told me a thing. How did you find out?" she asks.

"My mother bought me a douche syringe and she showed me how to use it," I say apologetically. Douching was mandatory. No decent married woman would think of not douching. I soon gave up the practice. Without douching, I thought I would die of disease. I thought somehow I would rot from the inside. I had been so scared into thinking that the sperm would be caught in there forever. My nurse friend hooted at me. The vagina is self-flushing. Douching will ruin your Ph balance. Don't bother. So I stopped douching. Like confession. I gave them both up at around the same time. I tried douching once after I had given it up, just like confession, and neither one did anything for me that I could tell. So I gave them up. Confessing to a priest was an exercise in futility. I had been humiliated by the old priest who was in our parish just before we married. My husband-to-be had to become Catholic in order to marry me. When we started dating in our Freshman year dad reminded me about religion and where the family stood on it.

"*C'est pas catholique, ça,*" he states. "He's not Catholic?" he asks to gain certainty after having made the statement. It was his way.

"No, dad, he's not Catholic, but I'm not going to marry the guy," I tell him at age fourteen. Disgusted. "We're just going to the Junior prom." Anybody could go to the Junior prom. As long as you bought a ticket and could afford a dress or suit. I had to ask his permission to go to the prom. And I was breaking with tradition. They had to meet my date. Everybody's else's parents insisted on meeting their daughter's dates. My parents were from the era that the boy or girl you brought home to meet the parents was the one you intended to marry. It meant you were serious enough about this person to introduce them to your parents. I don't know where they got these ideas. Some old French book of etiquette. I was bringing up father. And *maman*. So the first time I brought him home to meet them, it was for a Sunday dinner. *Maman* cooked one of her Sunday meal specials and then went into the bedroom to get all dressed up in a good dress. Dad went in to put on his suit pants, a white shirt and a tie. What was wrong with them? They did this for a fifteen year-old boy coming to supper. I was so embarrassed. They were going to scare the hell out of him. And none of my brothers were around. Everyone was married and gone on to live their own lives. No one was around to relieve the tension.

When, a few years later, we did begin to make plans to marry this boy and I, my father said he wasn't coming to the wedding unless the boy was baptized in the church. Dad meant what he said. He was a strong, French Catholic, almost as much as he adhered to the religion of alcohol, and no daughter of his was going to marry a Protestant. He stood his ground. Week-end alchy, or not, he was still the law in the house, and what he said went and I knew it. Did I have the courage to defy him on this one?

The boy and I continued kissing. I went in our parish church one Saturday afternoon feeling nostalgic about confession and its supposed cleansing powers. I was the only one in line. So I entered the confessional and oh, oh, too late, I see, it is "the old bird" as *maman* called him taking confessions this afternoon and not the nice, young priest with whom my boyfriend was taking his catechism lessons.

"Bless me, father, for I have sinned it has been (I lie) two months since my last confession." And more. I run through the prayer and list my sins. Swearing, lying, sassing, thinking unclean thoughts, doing unclean things with my boyfriend...

"Tell me what unclean things have you been doing with your boyfriend" asks Father of the "I want to build you a new church before this one falls on your head," and a piece actually does fall from the ceiling one Sunday evening mass and he stops the whole thing, which he is not supposed to do, and says, "See, I told you, this church is going to fall on you as you sit here! Give more money!"

I am afraid. I don't want to tell him. This old man. This celibate old fart who has probably never kissed anyone in his life, and who would want to kiss something as hateful as him. I tell him we touch each other.

"What!" he exclaims. All the composure and tell me you can trust me gone out of his voice. "You have to stay away from this boy! Give him up! Don't go near him!" The priest's voice has risen to a low yell. It echoes throughout the entire, empty, cavernous church. "Stay away from this boy. He is an occasion of sin!" he yells. "Give this boy up. You are sinning with this boy with your body which is the temple of God!" he goes on and on. He works himself into a lather. He reaches a peak, a crescendo in his denunciation of my sinfulness, my wicked woman ways. I'm thinking he is so out of touch with reality, it is just pitiful. Just pitiful. It is my only salvation. To feel sorry for him. In my mind echoes *maman*'s words, "poor devils" she'd call them. Sexless creatures she felt sorry for. *Maman* always had a strange notion of superiority based on certain things. One of which was she was not celibate. Father gives me my penance to say and a final "You have to give this boy up." And I am making up my mind that it is confession that I'm giving up. I'm going to marry this boy, fool.

I part the curtain and the only other person in the empty church is my sister-in-law. She is kneeling, praying, waiting to confess her young married life into the ears of the blasphemousness in the confessional booth. She sees me and goes in. She had to marry my brother. She was seventeen at the time and pregnant. She had to quit high school to get married. They married in the middle of the winter. I knew this at age eight. Later when I see her I try to alleviate my shame at being yelled at in front of her about my sexuality. She just waves her hand and puffs it off. Like nothing happened. She would not condemn me. She would not be the first one to throw a stone. "Forget it," she says with her hand and lips. That's nothing. By the way she dismissed the incident with her hands, she told me my desires were natural and I was not wrong to love my boyfriend. I stood absolved. I never told another priest anything about my private sex life ever again. None of them, in their public celibacy, what they did in private was their own business, *maman* said they kept women on the side and she didn't blame them, still, none of them deserved to know about my love life. Birth control included. Just as soon as the Vatican was willing to send me support payments, I may consider letting them tell me how many children we were to have. But since they were keeping their wealth in Rome, I was free to decide my own fate. I went to confession two more times after that incident, once the night before my marriage. I told the priest nothing. And, once again when I felt nostalgic. I came home and told my husband that it made me feel empty to tell a stranger my sins which I wasn't quite convinced of committing. So I gave up douching and confession in the same year.

The "Lightfoot" club of West Waterville have challenged the "Katahdin" club of Dexter to play a game of base ball on the grounds of "Ticonic" club, in this village on Saturday, September 10. The challenge will probably be accepted, as it was given after these clubs had played two games, in both which the Katahdins were beaten, but complained of the decision of the umpire in the second. The Lightfoot Club allow them to try again.

—*The Waterville Mail, Vol. XXV, No. 10, September 2, 1870*

Chapter 23
The Challenge Will Probably Be Accepted

One winter. Such a small space of time. Staring out of windows, being myself. Such a courageous act. No one to see me. No one to watch. The loneliness is crushing. I feel the snow swirling around outside and inside my head. Everything is swirling, swirling, swirling. I am surrounded by the deafening noise of silence and myself. I have only me to comfort and no one to comfort me. There is noise out there, the children are all talking and playing and being together, but I am forced to watch. Why am I always alone? I turn my back on the scene and return to my book. I've taken to taking my recesses inside. Alone. *Maman* doesn't know. Nobody knows my loneliness. I am crushed in my solitude. The air is hot with radiated heat. Winter slush is on the floor mixed with fine gravel. The seats in the classroom are all empty and recently vacated. The teacher, a man, comes back into the room to eat his lunch and mark the grades in the grade book. It will be a detail *maman* will ask me when she finds out I do not go out with the other kids at the noon recess. I don't want to stand against the building with no one to talk to me. I have withdrawn and I am comfortable in the withdrawal. I don't have to try. I can just let life wash over me and I can read myself into oblivion. I don't feel the pain of the loneliness if I read about Nancy Drew and her two best friends who never desert her because she is of a different age or has an accent. Nancy Drew does daring things and she eats the best foods, flies everywhere, and does it all. My son in later years, far from the loneliness of my childhood, deep into the years of motherhood, will call people like me "arm chair warriors."

It is a loneliness compounded by a home life steeped in alcohol and prescription medicine unhappiness. My father is at his worst these days. He is like a zombie. He hasn't touched *maman* in six months. Except to throw his slippers at her when *mémère* comes to stay with us for a weekend. Bad fight. *Mémère* called her other daughter in Dedham to come get her because she doesn't have to live with alcoholics anymore. Her husbands are dead now. Ugly and angry men are something *mémère* doesn't put up with anymore. So, she calls her daughter to come get her. My *maman* is shamed. She cannot have her *maman* come stay with her because dad is too ugly to let her have her *maman* stay with her. Even for just a little while. So tomorrow *mémère* will be gone and we won't get to see *mémère*. I am sad about that. I am very frightened because I never saw dad's eyes go white without any color in them when he was drunk or drugged before. He usually has sky blue eyes. This time they were the color of a huskie's. The snow has blown into the eyes of a huskie for so many years, the dog stopped fighting to keep the color in his eyes, he just let the snow blow in and whiteout the color of his eyes.

The color of his eyes. Oh, yes. I have never seen a boy with such blue eyes. Or, such black hair. His father acts ex-military and keeps his two boys' hair cut short. I'm in love. He is two grades older than me, but I am very mature. Unhappy, but mature. Silent in my love as anything else. I watch his every move and habit. I am eleven and he is thirteen. He goes to smoke at the small store near our country school. He only wears a white tee-shirt and black pants. Sometimes he wears a pork-pie hat. I know my men by the hats they wear. All the men I will fall in love with will wear hats. Or hats like his. Lonely, sad, silent, shy, over-bold in moments of stress, loud to cover up the sweats, pits dripping like faucets whenever he comes two feet near. He asks my very best friend to sit on the bus with him. She knows I love him. We are friends in the fall and spring of the year. In the winter she thought I was too young for her. In the summer which follows the spring and the fall of the following year, we are eternal friends. Blood sisters. *Maman* makes us matching tops for the field day. Handkerchiefs print tops. She wears a tee-shirt underneath hers because her bra would show. I do not wear a tee-shirt and my bra does show. The bra is yellowed under the arms because of all my nervousness and sweating. Always something to be embarrassed about. Breasts, bras, blood, bleeding. I have started my period at age eleven. It is proof to my eternal friend of my maturing. I have been bleeding since the summer before. She is not aware of this. In fact, I began bleeding before she did. She is jealous of my bleeding. The country boys go through the older girls' jacket pockets looking for sanitary napkins to play pass with at recess. They tease the girl mercilessly from whom they take her pad. She is only laughing, hands in her coat pocket, "Give it back, give it back." A curious form of courtship. These country people are so frank about their bodies. So open about their sexual selves. So many fall in love and moon across the classroom. There are four boys in love with me. I have never been so lonely and so loved at the same time. They expect me to love them back. I love only one and he has not told me he loves me, he only acts like he loves me. Like asking my very best friend to sit on the bus with him. He does this because he does not love her, they are only friends. She thinks my love for him odd.

Sharing secrets, I tell her one day who it is that I love.

"Him?" she looks at me askance. Nobody falls in love with him; he is too wild. Too crazy. The shyest girl and the wildest boy. Maybe she thinks I am too ambitious in setting my sights on such an older man. I'm too far gone to consider age. And besides, why would he ask her to sit on the bus with him if it was not just a ploy to get me to sit in the same seat as well? She is in a devil of a mood. I follow her down the aisle of the bus to go sit where he is standing and yelling: "Dee, come sit with me?" She goes past the seat a few steps and points out the seat to me. He is in the seat already and she means to make the sweating girl sit too close. I am shocked and nod my head no emphatically. I cannot speak. I am a mute. I am too afraid. She insists. She shoves me in and I fall against him. He has gone strangely quiet for the wildest boy as well. And then she sits and shoves me in further, right up against him. We touch and press sides, three to a seat, all the way to her house. He did not get off at his stop, but stayed on the bus for an extra hour to ride all around the bus route. His was supposed to be one of the first stops. He could even walk home if he wanted to, but he took the bus a few times. She gets off a few houses before mine. I push over and stay in the seat next to him till I get to my house. I mumble a good-bye. Too thrilled to forget the thighs and shoulders pressing for the rest of my life. I'm all charged up. The next time I press thighs with a man will be underwater with the man I marry. And the next time I press thighs again will be in a taxi cab in London. But this bus ride in Detroit was the first time I ever pressed thighs with a boy——man-cub.

The stone piers of the new bridge are finished and doing service. The work on the western abutment is progressing. If the planks are on hand we shall soon report the bridge passable.

—*The Waterville Mail, Vol. XXV, No. 18, October 28, 1870*

Chapter 24
The Bridge Passable

Falling in love at eleven and twelve feels wild. And I wonder if I really am in love. I mean, how is it that I can be a child and a woman at the same time? The outside shell is telling all kinds of lies to the world because the woman in me knows she is in love. She is too shy and silent to say so, but she is miserable. And ecstatic. Euphoric. And seduced, while seducing. The bunk about children and puppy love is some kind of adult superiority complex. Some way of feeling like a hot shot by making someone, a younger human, feel small and insignificant.

Still, I kept asking Dee, "Do you think I'm in love? Is this love? Do you think this is love?"

"How do you feel?" she wants to know.

"Sick."

"That's love," she replies from the wisdom of her thirteen years.

"Do you think it is only 'puppy love'," I worry.

"No," she is getting impatient with my worrying. I have to worry about the quality. This is my first love. I am proud of the boy I chose. There are others who are as sick in love as I am. I can see it on their faces when they look at me. Like they are ready to throw up with joy. Especially Charles. He is making me sick to look at him. He has such adoration in his face when he looks at me I am taken aback. I have strange notions because I read so much and odd, big words come out of my mouth. I am a strange kid to begin with. I have too many beautiful clothes because my *maman* is an expert seamstress and I am her only daughter. All the other girls have a few nice things to wear. I own a small store's worth of dresses, skirts, shirts and coats. Maybe fifty dresses and outfits. At least ten to twelve skirts. Several colors and weights of material. Some for the hotter weather and some for the cooler weather. I have clothes for the summer, fall and spring and a whole new wardrobe for the winter. *Maman* loves to sew. Her *maman* sews, too. All the *mes tantes* sew. *Maman* has a new zigzag sewing machine. She makes me dresses to fall in love.

We are in church. He is Catholic. Dad would approve of this one, except he's a wild boy. (Except I am not to have any boyfriends until I am sixteen.) Always in trouble. He gets the strap at school and then when he gets home, his father beats him again. Some days he is sullen from the beatings. His family sits in the back on the right at church. *Maman* makes us sit up front on the left. I can feel his eyes burning a hole into the back of my head all during mass. I don't dare to move a muscle. I think of him all during mass. I wait for communion so I can keep my eyes on him as he passes by. Today he is wearing a white shirt. He is too cool to acknowledge me. I can feel the electricity snapping between us. We are early to church today. Early enough to go to confession before mass begins. The priest is French like us. *Maman* speaks French to him. He has a limp. A war wound. He was a chaplain during World War II. He tells *maman* and dad stories about the war. He is a kind man. A giving man. For a priest. He is taking confessions before mass. I decide to go. I have gotten my courage up to walk in the church, the same church in which the boyfriend sits. Or, maybe I think he has not arrived yet. I get up to go to the back of the church. My minuscule veil, a round piece of black lace bobbypinned to my hair flies in the breeze of my walk. I am focused on the floor boards and walk straight ahead. I get to the back of the church where the confessional box is, and I see getting up out of his pew, is him, the lovely boy with those blue, blue eyes. I line up on my side because both confessional stalls are busy; he lines up opposite me because his side of the confessional is also busy. We can see feet kneeling underneath the curtains which divide the confessee, and the priest, confessor, is in the middle with his war wounded leg sticking out beneath the door. I am in shock. Caught. Once having decided to go to confession, I have to stay there standing in the back of the church across from the boy I love looking at me with equal love, and something like amusement, in his eyes. He is mocking me. I am mortified at his effrontery. His confessional stall is freed first. Ha! I am thinking, release! He will get out of my face so I can faint. He is motioning with his hand for me to go first. Like a perfect gentleman, he is letting me confess my sins before he confesses his sins. He is giving me his place in his confessional stall. I motion back that's O.K., no, no, you go first. I will not be outdone in politeness. The height of lovemaking—he is being kind to me. He is earnest in his love and will not be denied this chivalrous act. After you, he indicates. I feel like a queen. I am honored. I am flustered. I am confused. I am loved. I have proof of his ardor. He let me cut in line to confess. Why would a bad boy like him want to confess, I further reason. He would never have gotten out of his pew on his own to go to confession. He only did that so he could be near me. So we could be together. I obviously have influence over him. I could turn his life around. I could be his help and his salvation. We could be married and the perfect couple of 1963. We are teenagers in love. I confessed, but not with a clear mind and when I had come out of the confessional, he was no where in sight.

Rumble seats, hot rods, seats on the bus, kissing on the bus like I've seen some couples do. Except I will not pass half chewed M & M's like Dee and I watched one couple do. Sharing half-chewed candy is a bit much. We saw them kiss and exchange crushed, salivated chocolate. We told everyone the next day at school and then everyone else watched the kissing, chewed food exchanging couple the next day. We grossed them out with our comments on the spectacle they offered up for our viewing pleasure. The kids on the bus talked it through play-by-play—grammar school and high school kids all rode on the same bus. Wally's bus. The kissing couple only kissed, French-style without the food exchanges, from then on. They were angry at the little brats who dared to ridicule their love affair accented with half-chewed M & M's.

Father *L'Hiver*, formerly of Waterville, but now of Rockland, resembles his apostolic predecessors in one particular, sure——he is a good fisherman; and because we know it will interest his old parishioners, by whom he is held in kindly remembrance, we mention the fact that he lately hooked a four pound trout.

—*The Waterville Mail*, *Vol. XXV, No. 3, July 15, 1870*

Chapter 25

A Good Fisherman

It is the summer of 1964. There are yearly traditions in this country town of Detroit and the children or families prepare for them with equal parts of anticipation, excitement, joy, and now they have someone new to share them with—me. About each ritual, much is made of it. Talked up to proportions beyond my wildest dreams. The annual field day. Bazaar? No, field day. Games! Three-legged races, burlap bags races, softball games, no school! Everyone plays. Even the teachers. The Boy with the blue eyes wants to run a three-legged race with me. He laughs at my fear of him. He laughs at me, period. He just laughs whenever I am around. Smiles, is happy. Shines. Bubbles. Brews. Teases. Makes trouble in a kind way. Upsets my silences. Is ashamed when he is reprimanded in front of me when he causes too much attention to be paid to himself and the teachers scold him. Fallen from grace, rejected by society, to shy me, he is even more my hero. He tells the spinster teacher an insult and he runs away from school that day. I want to say something to comfort his pain and the most I can do is stare at my hands in my lap. Blush from over-awareness of his presence.

"Hey," he yells after me with my leg tied to Dee's for the three-legged race "Do you want to run the next race with me?"

I turn to look to see if it is really me he is talking to. It is! I'm almost as happy as if he had asked me to marry him. Or to be his girlfriend. Because if we did run a three-legged race everyone would see that I was his girlfriend. Boys and girls, in my sidewalk Catholic upbringing, don't tie their legs together and run races. That would be like getting engaged, for Christ's sake. I laugh. I'm not ready to be engaged. I'm twelve years-old. "No, thanks," I mock him back. He knows I would refuse, but he tries anyway. He is laughing and watching me run races. He has to content himself with that. I won't let him any closer. He cheers me on! I have never been bathed in so much attention from a boy in all my life. Back in the city where I come from, it is only the popular girls who have some-one love them. Not since the swinging wild jump rope days, have I had such joy flood my being.

He plays softball and his team wins. He is a good ball player. I cheer for him in my silence. I stand with my teammates and shine like a beacon of good will. I am sure I am electrocuting him with my feelings. He can see I adore him. From afar. I look around me and I see others talking to each other—guys and girls—and yet I am too shy to say a word. I can only glow.

During the summer of 1964 I became a woman in my own right. During the school year, those of us who were Catholic, had regular C.C.D. on Saturdays. C.C.D.—Confraternity of Christian Doctrine. I was the proud owner of superior knowledge about Catholic Church because up until the time we moved to the country to live out my father's collective memory of a farm, I had attended parochial school and I had memorized the Baltimore catechism. Several volumes. Going to Catholic school, I was extra holy and exempt from C.C.D. in the city. All my public school, catholic friends and neighbors in the neighborhood had to spend their Saturday mornings in my school, sometimes in my chair, while I stayed home and watched cartoons on T.V. Ha. Ha.

But now that I lived in the country and attended public school, I had to go to C.C.D. where the disturbed boy disturbed class. The teachers could not contain him. His sister was embarrassed by him. I found him too bold and much too aware of his penis. He in turn made all of us aware of his penis as well. We talked about his weenie almost all the time or listened to him talk about his weenie. He had a fat ass, too. So he seemed to be all genitals, and I thought in my girl thoughts that somehow this affected his brain. His face expressed he knew too much. He was a little older than all of us because he had stayed back a couple of years, and he held himself like he constantly had to pee. I was not amused by his antics and his fake stupidness. I told him so. I saw through his game. He wasn't much different than any other lecher I had met. Only he was younger. Not nice looking, and who would spend any time taking his acting out seriously deserved to get sucked in. I was not about to get sucked in. I told him to straighten out and fly right. Or wake up and die right. Or just plain drop dead. He was hurt by my seeing through his act. But he didn't try to pull any fast ones on me and we actually had some nice conversations. You could tell I did not care two hoots for this boy because we were pals. I was friends with his sister for a while. She and her family was from a suburb of Boston where many of my relatives were as well. So we talked about Boston and our latest trips there. We discussed traffic, crime, and the heat of the city. We were city slickers. We were in the sixth grade. Her brother joined us in our talk. They were also French. They had a French last name, but no language—verbal or body—was left in them. Their cousin was the one who loved me like a love-sick puppy.

A nun was coming to town, I was informed, for the Summer Bible Camp. Catholics didn't go to Bible camp, but in the company of Protestants who were the majority in town, the Catholic children were hard-pressed to describe to their Protestant friends the concept of studying religion in place of studying the Bible. The shortest route was to lie and tell the Protestants we were studying the Bible at camp just like they did. Except we don't go to a camp. We go to the church hall for a week. Every summer they get one nun who comes to teach them. One nun. They never see nuns otherwise. There are no Catholic schools for miles around and no convents in sight. They act like it is a big deal to get a nun for a teacher. I am bored by the prospect and act like it. Yawn. Nuns? We have them for breakfast, lunch and supper where I come from. And they usually are not very nice. Still, I get to get off the farm for one whole week everyday because *maman* drives me to Pittsfield for Bible camp.

I have to explain everything to *maman*. Everything is new and she doesn't trust what is going on. And there are boys where I am going. At the convent, she doesn't have to worry about boys or men being around, because the sidewalk crack keeps us all separate in Catholic children land. I go where the other kids go. Is the boy with the blue, blue eyes going to be there or is he going to be haying or something I wonder with deep, deep anticipation. I hope, oh I hope, he comes, too. I jump out of the Willy and scan the crowd of kids. I am disappointed beyond words. He is not here. Soon, his black family car with the correct license plate numbers drives up and he gets out. My heart jumps for joy. We all pile into the hall and sit in metal folding chairs. We sing. "If I Had a Hammer" and lots more songs. She is a nice nun. A young nun. A singing nun. A joyful nun. Wow. Where did they get her I wonder. I check out her habit. I wonder which order she belongs to. I start a rumor for someone to ask her for me. My friend asks her the question. She tells us which order she belongs to. Not the Ursulines. Ursulines are a teaching order. A strict order. A once cloistered order. My nuns used to tell us how their mother's funeral would pass in front of the convent and they were not allowed to attend. Things had changed they told us, but as children, we could see the scars on their hearts. Their personal sacrifice which was null and void in the face of the changes. This nun was never locked up inside of herself as the other nuns I had known. And she was happy and made us happy. Each child had a story to their name. There was sadness among all the children. We were all unhappy in some way. We made each other happy. As children we were a crowd, a community of country children moving on the landscape like a swarm of bees or a flock of birds. We belonged together and we were tied together by our four-room school house and the small village we lived in. We belonged because we belonged nowhere except with ourselves.

Poverty stricken. Native Americans. Dirt floor houses. Lack of soap and running water. Limited futures in common. Bookmobile library. Because we had so little we had so much. At Detroit Elementary, each thing we had or did was twice as rich and twice as celebrated because we had so little. Each small community event was twice a blessing because of the dearth of experiences. All things were magnified beyond its simple importance. A simple, country school field day with burlap bags, rope, some community people with stop watches and wire rim eye glasses, girls in pants and skirts, grape juice, baseball, summer heat, a new-mown field, a nun coming to town for a week, the Halloween party at the town hall, eighth grade graduation, Thanksgiving dinner served on the school desks gave a sense of place and belonging I had never had in my entire, unsophisticated life.

The nun asks us to tell her Bible stories. Real Bible stories. Not religion regurgitated, but stories about Jesus and his buddies, Adam and Eve, and more, like Noah. It was like a test of what we knew about the Bible. Some stories we didn't know. I knew all of them. Boy that was strange. I didn't think I knew the Bible, only the Baltimore catechism.

"Who can tell me the story about Adam and Eve?" she asks. That's an easy one. Everyone knows the story of Adam and Eve. We've been paraphrasing the Bible this morning in childish lisps or fake woman and man voices. All ages are at Catholic Bible camp. Sitting on metal chairs. The blue eyes are sitting just two rows in front of me in the very first row because he's earned himself a front row seat with his tricks. I am in the third row and there is no one sitting between us to spoil my view of the back of his head. He's not too tall, so that makes us the perfect couple.

He raises his hand as if to answer. I am intrigued at his audacity. This I've got to hear. The bad boy is going to tell Bible stories. I am laughing to myself. He is going to tell us the story of Adam and Eve, the first man and woman God ever made. The ones who started the whole thing. The ones who ruled the Garden. And they in turn made the first babies. And they lived together. They walked around without any clothes on. Till Eve took a bite of that apple and offered some to dumb Adam, who also took a bite and then God came into the garden to see them. And God said "Hey, Adam, where'd you go?" And Adam crouching behind the bushes with Eve, squeaks out, "I'm here, God." And God asks, "What's wrong? Why don't you show yourselves?" "We're naked," Adam says. "Who told you you were naked?" God wants to know. "We ate of the forbidden fruit," Adam admits. So, God made them some clothes out of fig leaves and told Adam he was going to have to work hard to get the Garden to grow and Eve, well, Eve, having babies was going to be painful from now on. God kicks them out of the Garden and sets up Michael the Archangel to watch with a flaming sword just in case they try to sneak back into the Garden at night to steal some fruits or something and God hides the door to the Garden so everyone forgets where God put the Garden. The whole thing in the Garden of Eden was a set-up I think to myself daydreaming, talking to myself as usual.

Old blue eyes is waving his hand crazy and wild in the air for the nun to see him. She turns to him to acknowledge his hand waving, asking permission to speak. He turns to me, points and says: "She can tell us the story of Adam and Eve." He completely turns around in his chair, puts his chin on his hand resting on the back of his chair, waiting, ready, to watch me tell the story of Adam and Eve. It was years before such a perfect seduction ever happened to me again. If ever.

We have had it in mind for several weeks to move a vote of thanks to the proprietors of the several tenements in *Boutelle* Block, for the general "slicking up" of their fronts, which has improved the appearance of the Block very much.
—*The Waterville Mail, Vol. XXIV, No. 17, October 28, 1870*

Chapter 26

"Slicking Up"

I dreamt the other night that I was a brownie, the cake mix kind, looking for some points. I dreamt this phrase. I was thinking about literary unmentionable acts such as housekeeping. Housekeeping as a way of making one's way through one's own dirt. I used to be a housekeeper for a man, an old French family in the South End who had had a furniture store on the Kennebec River bank which had escaped the hazards of urban renewal. In fact, the furniture store was like the last lone-standing ghost in a town where life lived had happened. Remnants. That's what I could feel when I walked into the furniture store to collect my pay for cleaning house for M. *Pomeleau*. He was ponderous. He had a penchant for canned gravy. Every night. On top of everything. He would open a can and pour it on and enjoy his cooking.

I got the job after Bunny was tired of working as his housekeeper. Bunny had more confidence than me so she got a real job working in a nursing home. I interviewed with M. *Pomeleau* at the furniture store. I was teenager confused; I saw the world through a haze of half-heard things and unclear thoughts which made the world mine. I could design any reality to fit my latest craze. I was still in my interior decorator stage. I had read a story about how a young woman got her own apartment and decorated it herself. With the help of an interior decorator. Nobody on Water Street employed the services of an interior decorator, but I thought I might like to be one. So I told M. *Pomeleau* that I would be an excellent housekeeper, which to my ears translated as: interior decorator. I had notions about what I could do with his house to "fix it up." M. *Pomeleau* was a widower. Lonely. His wife had died years before. He had been alone ever since. I was hired to rescue him from the accumulations of our daily dust and more. Obviously, I thought, after I saw his place. It looked like a woman had not been inside the house for years. And years. I found a snapshot of a woman sitting at the kitchen table with a kerchief wrapped around her head. With a beer in front of her. Happy. She, I could tell, would be upset if she saw what a mess the place had become. I was here to honor her death by cleaning the house, that I could see in the photo, was much, much cleaner than now.

I talked to Bunny at school. What had she been doing for M. *Pomeleau?* How come the place was still so dirty? She shrugged her shoulders. He told me to do the dishes and wash his clothes and sweep the floor. Scrub the toilet. Change his bed and make it again. Dust. So I did. She told me.

Matter of fact. Bunny was matter of fact. I was over-reactive. I began to rave. Did you see the cat and all the cat hair? The grime on the cupboards? Poor man. Neglected for all these years. Wife dead. I think I have my work cut out for me. Bunny said he really only wants you to keep the place up. I wasn't listening. I was thinking of paint samples, color swatches. Furniture groupings. But first the *Comet* and *Clorox* bleach. Phew!

The Sister of Charity who is nursing Marshal McMahon says that he never uttered a complaint during the dressing of his wounds. No matter how they cut and hacked in the frightful wound, which completely traversed his thigh, and in which a boy ten years old might turn his fist around, not a groan was heard. Whatever is given him, whatever is done for him, his reply is always, "Very well, my good Sister."

—The Waterville Mail, Vol. XXIV, No. 18 October 28, 1870

Chapter 27

"Whatever Is Given Him"

Summer Street. M. *Pomeleau* lived on Summer Street I walk up Cemetery Hill, past the Dwyer Bus Depot Garage to get to his house. I am pushing to be grown-up and delivered into adulthood at age fifteen through the exalted role of the housekeeper. I had responsibility to attend to. I wanted to make my own money to buy my own art supplies so I could get a portfolio together so I could go to art school and become a famous interior decorator. I do the dishes while *Secret Storm* is on so I can see what Nicole is up to. Nicole disappeared from the soap opera that summer of 1969. Five years later when I was standing in front of my own TV in my apartment in Portland, after I was married, Nicole reappeared on the same soap. I had not missed a thing. She had just blown in from a storm from some deserted island. Ship-wrecked. Or plane-crashed. Nichole survived. The only one. I clean M. *Pomeleau's* house like I just blew in from some storm. I blow through that place like a surprise, not so secret, storm. In one day. I almost work myself out of a job. I come from a family of workers. Ethnic types for centuries scrubbing away the grime of the 'h'english h'aristocrats'. Except M. *Pomeleau* was not h'english, him. I use bleach and that green can of bathroom cleanser. All in the same house, but, lucky for me, not in the same pail. I scrub cupboards, walls, floors, toilets, bathtubs, kitchen sink, dishes, tables, doors, door knobs and more. I bleach the sheets, the blankets, and I scrub clean the kitchen chairs, the windows, stove, refrigerator, and counter tops. My *maman* would have been ashamed of me because she was no longer into the French woman's neurotic cleaning. She used to be, she would tell you, but now I have better things to do than scrub the walls and floors, driving myself crazy . Some of those nuts are always nagging at the kids: 'Take off your shoes, don't mess up the house.' Humph. I can't be bothered with that shit any more she'd say. I'd rather be working on one of my projects. *Maman* likes to sew.

So I clean and clean till I almost drop in my tracks. I walk home elated. Oh, I forgot to mention the interior decorator's part. I rearrange M. *Pomeleau's* furniture. The furniture which had sat in the same place for over thirty years, and, certainly, had never been rearranged since his wife had died. All shrines become permanent fixtures. The next day I attack the house with the same gusto. I make plans to paint and wallpaper and redecorate the place like it is my own. I start to explore the second floor rooms. What could I do with those rooms?

Well, every three or four days I walk down to the furniture store on Water Street to collect my pay. Six dollars or so. M. *Pomeleau* sits at a kitchenette set waiting for customers to come in. I can't say that there are that many customers, but I could tell from the way he was waiting for customers that at one time this had been a booming business. He looked a little tired. From my vantage point of the tail end of a cultural tidal wave on a town, I wonder how he stays in business. I almost feel guilty collecting my pay. And odd. I feel as if I am standing next to something which once had been great, but only a semblance of what it once was is sitting there. M. *Pomeleau* does not have to bother to try anymore to be a force. He's done all that. From my youthful place in the world, raring to be someone or something, I want to lay a stick of something beneath his butt. Stop smoking them damn cigarettes and cut that depression shit out. I'd seen his house. I recognized the lethargy which had set in.

Bunny saw me first after my cleaning spree. "Thanks for showing me up," she tells me.

What do you mean I ask from my haze of teenagehood. After all, I was a world famous interior decorator in the making.

You go into M. *Pomeleau's* house and clean and clean until it shines and he tells my mother what a good job you did.

Yeah? I was pleased to hear he was pleased.

You made me look bad.

I made you look nothing. I did what I do. You do what you do. I'm the housekeeper now since she had got a new job. How's the nursing home?

I went to collect my money from M. *Pomeleau* for the first time. He sees me coming and he starts to laugh. I haven't said a word to him and he is cracking up. First, he wants to know who my father is. Oh. He says. He knows him. Of course he knows him. Everyone knows everyone 'down the Plains.' Then he tells me of his adventures after the fact of my cleaning storm hit his house. He could not even sit at his kitchen table to eat his supper as he usually does he tells me. He had to go outside on his front porch to eat. But before he did that, he said, the minute he walked into the house, the fumes hit him. He had to open all the windows to air the place out. He was forced to eat his supper and to sit on his porch all night long. He noticed I had changed the furniture all around. Told me about his wife and how nothing had been moved around since she had died. And here I go in the place, not asking permission or anything, high on my fantasy of interior decorating, rearranging his life. He was a man in his 50's at least. Maybe 60's. That is how I learned that men don't always care to have their furniture moved around. But he told me he liked it. He liked the couch at that new angle. I must have felt like a tidal wave coming into his gravy-laden life. We settled into a routine he and I for over a year and a half. No boyfriends he told me. I was not to bring in any boys. I wish I knew some I think to myself. I toned down on the interior decorating routine and did my chores in habit formation. We talked about paint once or twice. But mostly, my battle was against years of pre-existence. I'm sure that the minute I left, whatever smells or previous life-times that had existed, took over once again.

M. *Pomeleau* was a good-natured man. *Un géant. C'est fin cette l'homme. Fin* means the kindest possible in a human being. I was always bringing someone or something new to challenge *maman* and dad. They were a little surprised when I told them I was going to be a housekeeper. I didn't need to do dat dad said. You'll be working all your life. Yeah, but I want to buy some art supplies and they are expensive. And I want to buy them myself. I did not want to feel obligated and I wanted to be independent. Dad knew the family of *Pomeleau*s I was going to be working for. They used to do business with that furniture store. Dad had to know if it was safe for me to be with M. *Pomeleau* in his house. Dad went down to the furniture store to talk with M. *Pomeleau*. I felt very safe with M. *Pomeleau* and besides, he was never around when I was there cleaning. I would clean house for *maman* in the morning and after lunch, I would walk up the hill to M. *Pomeleau's* to clean his house. One day I changed my habit and I went in the morning. It happened to be raining that day and I did not see that the kitchen light was on through the window. I opened the door and there he sat in his usual spot at the kitchen table. I turned to close the door and swear to myself. I did not like to be in the house cleaning when he was around. As I am facing away from him to close the door, he barks out an order: "Don't turn around!" I'm thinking if he does anything to come near me, I'm going to blast him. I do as he says. I hear him walking, but towards his bedroom, not towards me. Still, I am facing the door and not able to see what is going on behind me in the room. I have no idea what he is up to. Maybe, I think to myself, I should open the door and run home to tell my parents. But I stay a few more seconds. Soon I hear a zipper being zipped. "Okay. You can turn around now," he laughs. "I like to sit around in my shorts," he said, "you surprised me by walking in without knocking. The only thing I could think of doing so you wouldn't see me in my underwear is to tell you not to turn around. I had to think fast," he says this like he is very pleased with him-self. I let out a big sigh of relief. Men did not sit around in their underwear in my house unless it was hunting season. Then they would sit around in their long johns. Not even when dad was drunk, did he wear just underwear. He would go shirtless, drop his suspenders to the waist, but never did I see my father sit at the table in his boxer shorts. Who wore boxer shorts back then but very old-fashioned men? That and tank t-shirts. These were clothing items that belonged in the 1930's. Gangsters wore those things. Fedoras and spanky shoes. Not M. *Pomeleau*. Didn't bother him if it was 1969. For him, time was suspended. Except for his dishwasher.

M. *Pomeleau* always wanted me to use his dishwasher. One of the few in our neighborhood. He would notice the dishes draining in the dish rack. I'd go down to get my pay to buy me some oil paints or some paint brushes at the art supply store and he'd say: "Use my dishwasher." Over and over again. He was proud of the dishwasher. What he didn't understand was that I always timed my work—the dusting, sweeping, laundry, bed changing, around the dishes and dish washing. When I cleaned I would listen to the radio, Age of Aquarius crystalbluepursuasion youbabynobodybutyou sky pilot…but when the right time came—it was the soaps and me. *Secret Storm*, Nichole, and Ivory Dish Soap. You get the picture.

A drunken fight at the door of Lashu's saloon, on Thursday evening, attracted special attention from one of the policemen. One fellow came very near being arrested by a blow under the eye. Luckily the row did not spread far enough to frighten any of the officials. If the liquor holds out there is to be a second heat on the same track.

—*The Waterville Mail,Vol. XXIV, No. 5 July 29, 1870*

Chapter 28

A Second Heat
on the Same Track

Have you noticed at the storm's end that the birds sing once again? Song absent from your life leads to an silence which cannot be described. Traditional song. How did I miss that one? They may have been millions strong at Woodstock, but in my world we heard about those goddamned hippies from the TV. *Des Moudgits Fous et ses Folles. Moutagi. Moutard.* Shit-a-goddamn. I am definitely out of the mainstream or the coldstream. I read the newspapers and I see that Mrs. Joseph P. Kumquat of the Garden Society planted flowers in the front of the City Hall. I'm in the eighth grade and I complain to *maman* about the women's missing names. "Nice job, Joe." My *maman*'s name is *Rita Côté*. Pronounced in French: RhEETAH! CoTEH! Emphasis on the "ee," "tah" and "teh." Sometimes when she pays the light bill she's Mrs. Gerald R. Côté, but *maman* is no society matron so she has a first name which is plenty fine for her. I'm telling you, me. 'A real genuine,' she always said about someone who was putting on airs. Which sounded like, ah rheal jenyouwine, very drawn out. Like my *maman*, I'm outside of the garden society ladies circle so to me planting flowers in public places seems frivolous and then getting their picture in the paper besides is even more hilarious. Why don't they plant flowers at home? What must their husbands say? I wonder what garden society women talk about. I try to imagine their meetings or their conversations.

"This meeting will now come to order," Madame President, Mrs. Robert says.

"Ladies, ahem, we have just received our new seed catalogs," reports Seed Chairman, Mrs. Eldred.

"I was thinking that we should buy fifty geraniums at the new florist in town," replies Woman-in-Charge-of-Live-Plants, Mrs. Kenneth.

"That would leave me the task of obtaining seedlings for the park," exclaims, Mrs. Henry, the only college graduated botanist among the pack.

"Oh, have you all seen my daisies?" asks Mrs. Fred.

And more to that effect.

Bras were something else.

"Up-lifts!" dad would shout, drunk and jealous if *maman* went out to buy new bras that day. "You spent MY money on up-lifts!"

"Ah!" she'd exclaimed, shocked. "Aren't you ashamed? You filthy mouth. Don't talk that way in front of your daughter. *Enfant chienne.*"

I sat there thinking up-lifts was the oddest name for a bra that I ever heard. I said it to myself on the way to the convent for the next few days. Over and over again weighing the word in my mind. Up-lifts. Up-lifts. Up-lifts. Up-lifts. Up-lifts. Up-lifts. Up-lifts. Up-lifts. Up-lifts. Up-lifts. Up-lifts. Up-lifts. Up-lifts. Up-lifts. I'd look at the nun's chest and wonder if she was wearing any up-lifts. I wondered if anyone could see the pictures in my mind or my thoughts. Up-lifts. Up-lifts. Up-lifts. Up-lifts. Up-lifts. Up-lifts. Up-lifts. Up-lifts. I'm forty-two years old and I'm still contemplating how that word connoted nasty to my father. Or my mother.

That was mild compared to some of the things he used to say to her when he was drunk. The themes of his anger were predictable. New bras and girdles pissed him off. When she got a new permanent in her hair we would definitely hear about it. Sometimes all night. He used to pull all-nighters. But we knew when he was just about ready to go to bed because he would fry up some onions and hot dogs. Decades later, sitting in a Yugoslavian coffee shop in London, women in kerchiefs waiting on us behind the counter, serving us the best coffee I've ever tasted, being yelled at by a very small man frying up hot dogs and onions on the grill—I see visions. I have true *déjà vu*. The French kind, not the dejavoo of the English. I cannot tell anyone around me about the horrors of living with a drunk and the relief of smelling fried hot dogs and onions. All greasy and burnt. In London, I ordered two. And then we went back to the very same place the next night for more coffee and more fried food. I love dancing on bad memories. Like making up my own songs with the old lyrics rearranged.

In the earlier days, when he would call her from the mill two or three times a day to check up on her, the milk man, the mail man, the newspaper delivery boy, neighbor men—both at home and at camp were prime suspects. He accused her of having affairs with them all. He stopped the milk man from coming to the house. We could get our milk at Ted's, the corner store. At camp, he couldn't stop the men from looking over our way so he planted extra trees, hemlocks of all things, deadly poisonous, to screen her from view. Insanely jealous, he punched a complete stranger right in the face at the movie theater because he thought that the man had looked at her. He would scream at her about his money. Once he lined up all his guns, ten or so, up against the kitchen counter, to warn her that he meant business. I used to have nightmares. I transferred my fear of a frightful man to a boogie man who lived in the attic. He wore a trench coat. Dark-skinned. He had to be small because the door was not even five feet tall and it opened onto my bedroom. The latch was on my side, but any minute now, he would come bursting out and he would finish me off. I steeled myself against the boogie man. He wasn't any music maker either. Dad would swear and shout up the stairs as his music played loud on the record player. Drunk songs I call them now. The Singing Nun—*Dominique, nique, nique.* Johnny Cash. Something about red sails in the sunset. Had he told her lately that he loved her? A couple of songs from WWII and the German woman torch song—*Lili Marlene.* The sound of a certain song can bring back such memories of me and *maman* huddled upstairs on my bed, shivering from fright, diarrhea, and praying to God to please make him stop yelling. Dad would be mad about his quality of French background vs. her quality of French. *Une moudgite Aroostooke!* Your people are no good. Your mother was stupid. She never took care of the bunch of you. You all starved during the Depression. Now, there's a really good reason to hate someone, I think to myself, because they had no food during the Depression. My French is better than your French. *Moudgite Aroostooke.* And she'd yell some insults back which would keep him going for another hour to top her insults. I would plead with the one I thought I had the most influence with to try to get her to shut up. Shhh. Shhh. Don't answer him I'd tell her at eight and nine years old. He can't argue with himself. She used to stay downstairs with him and fight back. Now, she got away from him. So he couldn't hit her. Except he hadn't hit her for awhile. Not since I went to get the neighbors to break it up. And then everyone was ashamed of him being seen hitting her, so they told me not to do that ever again. Don't ever go get the neighbors again. So I didn't. I went to get my aunt who wasn't a neighbor, but a relative. The next time I called the police.

He'd be talking church and at the same time he'd *crêvé toute un fifth de whis-key.* Côté's Fifth. Drank the whole fifth. By himself. Tired and pissed off from the mill and taking it out on us. All the boys were gone and so that left the women to take the heat of the pressure of the mill of this sixth-grade educated man who was being eaten alive by the so many pounds of pressure per square inch at the factory. Our lesson for the evening would be the Acts of Faith, Hope, and Charity. *La foi, l'espérance et le charité,* which of course, we lacked. Everything he said to her I took upon myself. So, if we were at camp and he said: "I'm going to take you to the middle of the lake and trow you in," to me that meant we were both going to be drowned. Neither of us could swim. The threats became the code by which we lived. Mostly in fear.

When we ran away once, my *maman* took me to the local "horse" doctor to have a wart burnt off. I had hit it again and it was bleeding. Crying I was insisting on some kind of loving and I figured that my hurt would be taken care of in the doctor's office. He burned the wart off with a heated iron rod. She broke down and cried in the doctor's office telling him her troubles. Doctors were still the community counselors back then as well as the priests. You gotta stay with that man. Sleep with him. You are his wife! That was the priest's point of view which included: It's Your Sacrifice. Offer It Up To God. And then *maman*'s favorite: Your reward will be great in heaven. The doctor was much more creative in his advice. He told her that if she left him, if she got a place of her own, she would wonder at every footstep in the hall. She would wonder if he would be coming after her. So we stayed so she could keep track of his foot steps. I never smelt anything so bad as burning flesh in all my life. Except, much later when they would come to burn off the top beaks of the chickens in the chicken barn when we lived on the farm. That was the very same smell as my burnt skin. After the team of workers had immunized all the chickens and burnt their top beaks down so they could not pick each other to death, I would be sick from the smell of burnt flesh for days. And I would remember the hell of my father's angers. It's a wonder I never noticed Woodstock. And dad never taught me the traditional songs of our people. Not in the land of forgetfulness and stupor brought on by self-hate that he was taught to believe about himself.

The number of things to which the principle involved in the Frenchmen's recipe for *"cotelettes a la Metternich,"* can be applied is incalculable. "You have only to broil them like ordinary cutlets, and call them *'cotelettes a la Metternich'* when you serve them."

—*The Waterville Mail, Vol. XXIV, No. 10 September 2, 1870*

Chapter 29

The Frenchmen's Recipe

The larger picture of life is designed to make you doubt yourself, or worse, go crazy. That's what he did. He took on the surrounding climate and he lost it. Rather he held onto his reality with the barest of grasps never quite matching the world in which he was living. He came from the old country inside of himself. Instead of sticking to the recipe of what was best for him, my father, with a foot in two cultures, tried to re-write the recipe. But when the ingredients are not available, how can you keep to the recipe? All I have is my understanding from a vantage point of daughter watching a man struggle with his surroundings. Hearsay. Her say. I'm writing this on his birthday or what would be his birthday if he were alive. My dad died in 1984 on our daughter's birthday. His exchange child. He was born in 1916. I'm looking at the atmosphere of the city, a Maine-sized city, of Waterville as one of the places where the migration of French Canadians happened. They came to work and work they did. Some brought their shoes with them and some came educated, but all were not of the English recipe when it came to ways of being. So what happens to a man when his world does not sift right? And his woman and children? Some attempt adaptation. Some drink. But drinking for a French man is not the same thing as teetotaling wine sippers of the ancient enemy. When I was a kid we used to play army and the Hundred Years' War like it was yesterday. English meant Protestant; French meant Catholic. Those were the lines. You cross them and you go to hell. Life was easy to discern because Death was its constant companion. On a recent trip to the Southwest, leaving all the family behind me, I was companioned by Death. I realized being so far away from my children that death was more pronounced among us than life. I was more aware of my helplessness to protect them. The great separator of the quickened from the not so quickened. The world tends to scatter me to the four winds, directions, elements, corners and everything between. To get centered I travel mentally to the lonesome pine beneath which *maman* and dad are lying in the cemetery because there I can feel the magic. Beyond what I am presently beholding as reality, fades in comparison to my connectedness to the everlasting through my belief in seeing them once again. It is more than that. Whatever I am thinking or feeling has to have a reason for its creation or inception. I get meaning from standing by their shared tomb. Point of origin better than any compass can divine. These are ancient rituals which I am observing. Ancestor worship is among them. Wisdom palpable in the environment. The one ignored or shoved aside by the going deal of what's popular of the present.

That is the crime I charge. I charge the mainstream or popular culture with thoughtlessness and skimming over the sacred with scarcely a backwards glance. Ground underfoot. Overlooked. Ridiculed. Parodied. I accuse the ignorance of itself. Otherwise I don't know why else an ethnic culture would try to destroy itself wholesale. When day in and day out, the reminders are constant and unrelenting, subtle and barely seen, felt or heard at times and at other times, boldly proclaimed: "We don't take to your kind around here." The clash of the cultures. English-speaking and French-speaking. One word contains the DNA of the entire culture. One dominant and the other—goes underground. It does not cease to exist, because the face and fingerprints attest to their existence.

Dad had a face and he had fingerprints. Strong arms for a small man. Five feet six or seven tall. Triple EEE wide foot. Peasant stock. *Jean Côté* was the first *Côté* to emigrate to New France. When they had the *Côté* Family Reunion in Madawaska, Maine, my brother and I traced our lineage back to *Jean Côté's* son, *Noël*. The Christmas guy I call him. I'm looking for some let up from the damn melancholy. Dad couldn't remember the name of his *pépère* the time he tried to tell me family stories. We sat apart from all the other members of the family. We sat in the kitchen whispering to each other, talking in low voices because the others were in the living room ridiculing us. Hooting at my wanting to know the family stories and history. Self-hate is really big with the oppressed. Dad was hurt by their making fun of us, but I could see from the set of his face, he was going to tell me anyhow. When I came down to visit him the next time, he even had pictures to show me and he put them in a paper bag with my name written on it in his unschooled penmanship—misspelt. My father could not spell my married name.

Maman had died and I was living in Bangor. I got a call from him. You have to come to Waterville right now! *Bebite*. That is what he called me since I was a girl. *Bebite*. You have to come. Dad with his emphysema. The oxygen guy was due that afternoon and he had lost the list on how to spell the numbers from one to one-hundred *maman* had made him. He was going to have to write a check and he couldn't do it without the list of numbers. I tried to reason with him. Dad, call me when the guy comes and we can fill out the check over the phone. He would not be caught like that. The phone was right near where the guy would be standing and could hear everything that he and I would say. So I had to type him a new list, pack my three kids in the car and drive one hour to Waterville to give him the list of numbers spelled out. But this was not your basic illiteracy. This was bilingual. He could speak and understand two languages, but he barely possessed writing skills in either language. He went to the sixth grade till he was a grown boy well into his teens.

No one knows how much he depended on *maman* all his life and yet he abused her for the same length of time. But he always would apologize. And she forgave him. They lived the biblical seventy-times-seven math as forgiveness, as Catholics. French Catholics who never read the Bible a day in their lives, but had one sitting on the coffee table bought in sections at the grocery store each and every week. The same way she bought her dishes and her art. Van Gogh, Homer, Monet. For years I had a Van Gogh cardboard reproduction framed in my kitchen. The sunflower, and I had chosen it simply because I liked it. Some rock group had written a song about Van Gogh. A Japanese art student and his wife from Pittsfield came to visit me and my husband—leaving, she pointed to my grocery store art, and said with admiration like I had good taste or something: "Oh. Van Gogh." I had no idea. Life could pass you by like that and you never knew what had flown overhead. Or, under the radar. But the gut feeling about that flower remains to this day. That I know that Van Gogh painted it only burdens down my appreciation. Living culturally is like living by heart or eating garden grown fresh tomatoes; living self-consciously is like breathing hot-house air and eating the tomatoes grown there.

He told me when we were speeding to Lewiston once when my brother had hurt himself by making a Jim Bowie knife that he was afraid of my *maman*'s strength. *Maman* had told me he was afraid of her, but I had not believed her. What he was afraid of was his weakness alongside her strength. He fooled her into thinking he was the stronger one by terrorizing her into staying with him. Death beat him at his own game and Death collected his due. *Maman* left for heaven and dad was alone. He had learned from his own father how to keep his woman in the dark and from running away. *Pépère Côté* always threatened to kick his wife out of the house. The house and land which was deeded to her by her step-parents. Her own parents had died. He fell through the ice of the Kennebec one spring and his wife delivered a baby girl, Annie, my *mémère*, and two weeks later she died of a broken heart. Some bonds are too big to keep us down here. Maybe that is why I go to the cemetery. I want to be gathered up. Into the arms of knowing you belong somewhere that makes sense and that accepts you. Being French is just the wrong recipe, or they try to fake you out by serving you the wrong dish and telling you its the same thing as the original recipe.

The WAR—The French still insist that Bazaine's surrender was the result of treachery, while by some it is set down as part of a scheme for the restoration of the Bonaparte dynasty. The French people were also comforted for awhile by a report that the soldiers at Metz refused to lay down their arms and surrender at the bidding of the officers, but that was a mistake, for the Prussians are now in possession of the city and fortification.

—The Waterville Mail, Vol. XXIV, No. 19 November 4, 1870

Chapter 30

The French People Were Also Comforted For A While

A couple lying side-by-side in their graves can be seen as symbolic of a lifetime of living together. In Louisiana the graves are above ground because the water table is so high. In the seventh grade, Mother Star told us stories about Louisiana's graveyards. As a grown woman, I saw these aboveground graves—during a visit to Louisiana, one of the first places I asked my friend to take me was to see those graves so I could see with my own eyes what Mother Star had told us. She had lived in Louisiana as a young Ursuline nun. I see the graves and to me they look like double and single beds. Strewn about the countryside are these granite mattresses and pillows.

Mother Star told stories on Friday afternoons as a treat for our cooperation with her during the rest of the week. Monday morning she would announce from her dais: "Girls, if you do your work and everyone pays attention and we get this letter writing project done, on Friday afternoon, after the noon recess, we will spend the afternoon listening to story telling. By me."

The first time she announced this we were intrigued.

"I'm a very good story teller," she frankly said. "I have a special way of telling a story." Storytelling was for babies, not big girls like us. "Everyone loves my storytelling." she tells us. "Ask the girls who graduated. Ask the eighth graders." We share a classroom with the eighth graders. After being a student in this parochial school, getting to be the seventh and eighth grade girls means you are the Big Shots. You are special. You are Notre Dame Girls. You come from Notre Dame School and Notre Dame School girls always excel in the world. They are world famous. They do excellent work everywhere they go. You have a name to uphold—Notre Dame School—for the rest of your life. We believed them when they told us that. Only in this case, we are the Black *and* Blues Sisters from down on Water Street and we are on a mission from God, also. Nobody messes with us.

Louisiana graveyards are the bedroom of the dead. The eternal resting place. Graveyards—the bedrooms of America. After the fact. The stories she would tell. For three hours straight. From start to finish. Whole lifetimes, eras, cities, places in a woman who would hypnotize thirteen seventh grade girls in 1966 with story. Oral story telling. Words gained flesh. Story as only story can satisfy. Daily meanderings into intricate lives full of the stuff in graveyards. Not the spooks, but life. She told us the stories of ordinary people living the complexities of ordinary lives and then lying down next to each other for forever. Story as magic. Story as transcendence. Story as earth leaving. Story as mental rocket ship. Story as out -of-the-body. Imagination as key, fuel and passport. That's the best I can do today to recreate the magic of her storytelling.

If we knew what we were up against in reality, we might not have dared to dream. Some of us didn't. Some of us remained by the river bank to continue the tale of those who came to live there in the previous century. Some of us, cowards, left. We could not remain and fight for who we were in a place which told us we were no one or nothing. Our lives were unaccounted for before we were born. Ethnics on the fringe. Fringe dwellers. Breaking rules of the dominant society with rules of our own. Our ordered Catholic girls school lives was something much older than we realized. We are in the world of the hippies and we venerate the cross on Fridays during Lent just the same. We attend mass and we go downstairs to try to act like cool teenagers in a church-sponsored dance. The local, Catholic doctor, the hernia doctor, my "Doc," as *maman* called him, came to tell us about sex. In the basement, on the tiny stage. Boys one night and girls the next night. "Do you have any questions?" the man asked. Yeah, what did those dumb boys want to know? Who would even think of one of them as a serious boyfriend? We rejected all the boys in our class. They were too much like brothers. Oh, one caught my eye for a minute, but he slipped out of sight.

The story of the river bank dwellers went untold. Unless, of course, you go to the cemetery and start at the beginning. For yourself. Ask questions. How come all these French people are here? Who came to live here first? This is a very old place because I can feel the spirits of what once was here. M. *Pomeleau's* store will tell you that. And Mother Star, Mother Star could have told you.

"STAND BY YOUR ORDER." We copy the following appeal to the graduates of Colby University...A half century has elapsed since in a comparative wilderness, amid the tears and prayers of a few noble friends of education, this College was planted...From infancy oppressed with debt, denied the rich endowments which her sister colleges have so readily received, located in an unfavorable region...What are the duties of an alumnus to his Alma Mater?... What has the College done for him?...He came to her a youth; he graduates, a man fitted above others to fight successfully life's great battles, to exert a controlling influence in the affairs of men, to become a pioneer in reform... Graduates of Colby, have you performed your whole duty in this matter?
—The Waterville Mail, Vol. XXIV, No. 23 December 2, 1870

Chapter 31

Exert a Controlling Influence

I want to tell the story, but I'm afraid of the story. The story might eat me, or someone from within the story. I will be accused of telling the story from a wrong angle. I'm only one woman and I was sheltered in a runabout way. I had the run of my world, but I was kept out of other worlds. I gained only glimpses of those worlds. Riding by the mansions on the way to the hockey games. Hockey games held at the Alfond Arena at Colby College. The college that the alumni finally remembered and the college that fed off the town in workers and fed the town back with use of its ice hockey arena. Hockey as religion to the French. For both the women and the men. Five years old and sister to the star player. Today my son plays ice hockey. On the ice, the cultures converge—town and gown fade to GO Town! Hardly anyone goes to this college to go to school, but everyone goes to this college to play or watch hockey. Hockey players and their fans who know how to own an arena. A public permission to be great. Proud. French Proud. To be a winner. To be on the ice and to score. Hockey town. Our style. Everyone owns the ice. The rival hockey towns come to play and they are French towns—so the insults hurled are in French. The Catholic high school kneels on the ice by their goalie with their religious brother hockey coach. They play the dirtiest. Confession on Monday clears them of all blame. Coffee. Cold. Rituals. On the ice.

But the story is more than the sum of its stereotypes, and how we all love our stereotypes. The dumb Frenchmen on Water Street and his whores. Those loose women and their men. The women who clean their houses so clean that you can eat off their kitchen floor. Those mill workers *qui travailler fort toute son vie*. The *uneducated fous et les folles*. The wisdom inherent. Sanctioned lies embedded in truths. And before you know it, everyone is believing the lies. As truths. Even though they know it to be otherwise. Much more complex, and yet, willing to go along with the liars. Just to shut them up. The power of the story is with the one who tells the story and names the characters. The liars are both within and without as long as the story remains buried or hidden from view and not told in its originality. And every storyteller would tell a different story.

As my work waits for me, or other parts of my life insists on my presence, I sit here hoping to tell a story that refuses to be told and believed. How do you tell about drunkenness and not moralize or plan reform? The missionaries on the hill ready to transform the heathens at the bottom of the hill—tiers away from mutual experience. Waves of migration and funneling the migrants into the neighborhood and the mills. Aspiration and imagination shied away from, and disengaged from, the engine of reason. You are not supposed to be creative. You begin to swear at yourself. What could you possibly be thinking? Who would read this story? What can you say about a community of people who cooked, defecated, had children, had more children, prayed, neglected their Easter Duty and went to hell as a result, observed the Holy Days in taffeta and then turned whore soon afterwards because there was a price on their heads that the environment demanded? Most were poor, others polished their linoleum till they wore out. My family invested in inlaid tile, with a design built in the middle. A diamond shape in the kitchen and a star in the bathroom. Kitchen art built to last. Permanent artful utility. Maman canned 100 jars of corn to keep up with dad's *jardins*. The tomatoes, carrots, string beans—green and wax—*dans cave*. *Mémères*, both their *mamans*, had done the same. Canning and preserving the food from the gardens, fields and barns. *Une bonne boudjon*. A good broth. Dad would talk about broth with the meat like it was bottled gold. The remnants of the old country in collective safekeeping. Each carrying a piece, but the whole never intact. The French and their love of a good sauce. M. *Pomeleau* and dad could talk canned gravy and a good broth all night. That creativity.

The French of Water Street had their ways. Some kept their soup pot on to boil with the stewed tomatoes and onion. Hot and steaming, fragrant even if you didn't like tomatoes whole. Maman ground hers with the food mill. My generational connection was to continue grinding my tomatoes in the food mill given to me by maman as a wedding present to make my tomatoes fine and seedless. It was a way of showing I was not without a sense of good taste. Whole tomatoes were the sign of a lazy cook. All was well as long as we did not try to overflow our boundaries too much. As long as we kept our place. The program of keeping us in line was a subtle form of privatizing. Belonging to a separate race of men and women meant we could be rediscovered and reformed into the image of our maker. Full of guile, Catholic, swearing, sexed, colorful, shitting in public on Main St. in front of a bank one of us, and bringing shame to those who attempted to crash headlong past poverty, sewing as a marker of freedom and beauty, pipe fitter by ingenuity when nearly illiterate, machinist, janitor, maid, earnest, hard-drinking, bare-fisted, virgins and whores alike knocking on heaven's door.

I can tell you a story of driving on the narrow streets.

As a sophomore in high school, where admitting to living on Water Street is the shame of a lifetime accumulated in a crimson moment, my driving teacher asks: "Who knows which street in Waterville, the only street in Waterville that has a 20 mph speed limit? Somebody in here must know," he tells us. "I know someone in here lives there."

He goes around the room querying us. I sit there innocent, unaware my throat, troat, is about to be slit and all my social life's blood will be slipping from my body, proclaiming to the world, "Unclean!"

"You," he points to me, "you, don't you live on Water Street?"

Cornered, I nod yes. The power of place to destroy. I stand accused of my home. From the ancient of days and hours, the mortified rise in protest, swirling, swimming before my eyes. The shame of a nation falls on my shoulders. I am the fallen woman. I am Miss Scarlet A to Z. This is no frivolity. This is banishment and shunning. This is the mark of Satan and his cohorts. This is a day of rejoicing in hell. One more for Gehenna. I look this unsuspecting, uncaring, hardened innocent criminal in the eye and mutter: "Yes." Wounded, he cuts deeper, he chides me for not knowing the speed limit on my street. I have never experienced a more heartless human in my life.

"What's the matter with you?" he taunts "Haven't you noticed the speed limit signs?"

Embarrassed is a word you use when you can recuperate from your loss. Reprobate reaches my consciousness on this issue of admitting in high school as to where I live. And reprobate I shall remain all my live-long days. I was taught this hatred of place. I was told and I believed the telling of my dishonorableness. I vowed to return. In story. This used to be a story of revenge. A tale I vowed to tell when I was sixteen "to get back at them." Them who put me on this earth in such a place. A hell-hole with an ordinary aluminum screen door as entryway. Reprobate and the daughter of reprobates. Deviants of society. Escapees from a forgotten land relocated on land that would just as soon forget as well. The poverty of not knowing who you are is shame. The generations' lapse of memory. A people with no fuse box. No batteries. None even sold separately. Just douse yourself with alcohol and light a match for all we care. Women as pencil sharpeners. Use once and discard humans, or until they wear out, whichever comes first. Folded, bent and mutilated and believing every second they deserve it. Their children a repeat performance. Proud and elegant, but diverse in their expression. Drunk and prayerful existing in one man, and not drunk and exquisitely dressed, but swears, existing in his woman. Some poor to the point of begging. Deep and intelligent just the same.

I have come to love the story and the people of the story. I am reprobate still, but this is not a moment of decline. This is a moment of story telling and weaving my story into influence of a different nature. A reknowing ourselves on the land. The holy land of the river bank. Reaching all the way back to the homelands in memory. And back again.

The Pretty operetta of "Roneka, the Forest Queen," written by a young lady of our village, and performed by a few of her musical friends, had a flattering reception of three successful evenings. This is compliment enough for both the authoress and her friends—all of whom seemed to share the pleasure of the audience.

—*The Waterville Mail, Vol. XXIV, No. 22 November 25, 1870*

Chapter 32

Evenings

"Je te le dit jamais, jamais, mettez une fourchette dans mons panier, encore. Jamais encore." I am eight years old and we have gone to the mill to get our man. He gets in and as she drives away, it is Friday night, he begins to yell.

"Never, never put a fork in my lunch basket ever again!" he hisses.

She looks at him. Has he gone nuts? She's not aware of the seriousness of what he is saying. She laughs.

"Dey laughed at me because of dat goddamned fork dat you put in my lunch basket with dat piece of pie." he growled. "It was you who did dat to me," he warns her. "You." She is silent now. She knows she is in trouble.

The men at the mill punish one another and keep each other in line with insult. Or ridicule.

He is screaming at her all the way home. They cross the bridge over the Kennebec. The water rushes over the dam. I can barely see it from the height at which I sit in the back seat. I look forward to seeing the water rush over the dam every trip across the bridge.

He describes to her his encounter with the fork and the men. He holds her hostage to his wounds.

"I went down to eat and dey start in on me: 'hey, *Côté*, did your wife gif you a fork to eat your pie,' he imitates their cat-calling, braying taunt. In other words *Côté* is pussy-whipped. A weenie. A fairy.

"All de time I am eating my pie wid yor goddamned fork dey say to me, '*Côté's* got a fork.' Sonofabitch." He is almost white with anger. "Dey were laughing at me." We all fell into his black hole.

I'm eight years old and I'm listening about the men in the mill. I make my mind up to never, never marry a man who works in a mill. Later I say to *maman*, "Something is wrong with those men in the mill. They are all crazy. Like there is a secret society to be mean or something. Treat your wife bad." In my child's mind I thought that there was a club. A secret club and they made pledges to go home and beat their wives or to yell and scream at them all night about stupid stuff. I made up my mind. My husband would never have a chance to belong to such a club. If he did, I'd make him quit or tell them he wasn't interested.

"What are you talking about?" *maman* asks.

"Remember the fork?" I reply.

That night dad yelled and yelled about the men and the fork. All he kept yelling about was the fork in his lunch basket and how they laughed at him. His voice was a high pitched wail like an animal with its foot caught in a trap. He had been splayed open by the simple eating utensil. Already crushed in himself, he could not withstand anymore crushing and, in turn, we had to be crushed. Pecking order. His shame became our shame. Or our confusion. It is difficult to accept that a common fork was a weapon to destroy a man's reputation in mill culture. Your whole image depended upon whether you ate your pie with a fork or your fingers. Being vulnerable was a deadly mistake to your ability to bully your way out of the bottom of the heap. I don't know if *maman* ever put a fork in his lunch basket with pie again. But I remember the night of his yelling his humiliation about the time that she did put a fork in his lunch basket.

Years later when my husband was working his way through college by working in a paper mill, I had put a fork in his lunch basket to eat his pie just as *maman* had done. The same thing happened to my husband in a different mill in a different town. More than twenty years after the fork was the shame of dad, my husband was taunted in the same manner. Newlyweds they said she'll be giving you plastic forks in a few years or maybe none. My wife would never give me a stainless steel fork in my lunch…on and on. My husband just laughed. I couldn't believe it when he told me that they had laughed at him because I had put a fork in his basket.

Annie Russel, Keeper of a bagnio in Water street, was claimed to be the wickedest woman in New York. Owning to the efforts of missionaries Annie had been induced to break up her bagnio and send away the abandoned girls who violated the peace. Annie sent for one of the missionaries herself and when he visited her she said to him, "My God! I can't stand this life any longer." The reformed woman has been kindly cared for at the "Home for Women," and great confidence is expressed in her reformation."

—*The Waterville Mail, Vol. XXIV, No. 26 December 23, 1870*

Chapter 33

Wickedest Woman

The pressures of our common existences keep us in place. Otherwise we would be flung to abandon. Delicious, unkempt and open-minded abandon. Your best and worst fantasies would come true on a make-shift stage. The local bar and grill would redecorate and invite you down for one more time around. The nude dancers have long since vacated the premises, but their bump and grind is in your face. Still.

I am afraid of the shadows in my mind. No doubt about it, but I am willing to find out if it is true. True that in the woman lies her right to own her true nature. The one snatched away in fear that the environment will have its way with her and she will be carrying one, two or even three illegitimate children. She, and only she will be held accountable. The shame of the woman, the blame of her, is sex. Even in these days of post-The Pill. Double standard stands. Now I know, a voice must be spoken from where its source lies. From the point of the beginnings of her life. The reason why we all return to the scene of a crime. To understand its meaning. What hurts must be salved. Soothed. Even the joy of a place is pain disguised in its Sunday best. I'm sure of it. We enter this world on the point of pain and we leave it in the same manner—painfully. Our lives are steeped in the pain of being. Our attempts of assuaging that element of the essence of being is how we devise living. Some have more say about their boiling point than others.

We are the choices we make. But what choice did I have to be living in the household I grew up in? What piece of me agreed with the sea of alcoholism that I was tossed about on for the better part of eighteen years? What did that feel like to me a girl in a household of a tortured and wounded man who tortured and wounded the rest of us? Was he wicked? I cannot say that. There is no formula response. What of reform? We made pilgrimages to Canada to the holy shrines there. The homeland. The homeland closest at hand. Going back to the beginning for him. Canada. *Québec*. God. To get at meaning. And nobody knows the answers. The very things I needed for the life I was to lead, I learned in my earlier life. The ones who were supposed to not hurt you, did. They let me know early on that this world would be rich in pain. I would be hurt and don't be crying about it.

This leaves me open to misinterpretation. There are tea cups of solitude and moments of self-realization which leave us aware of other worlds happening in parallel to our own. There are visible worlds and hidden meaning in others. The myth is that the talking is the doing. Scary when you realize more is said in silence than bathos of double-speak. For a woman, and particularly for a woman of a culture which is out of sync with the dominant currency, she is put to the stake twice for burning—once for being woman and another for being born in the wrong ethnicity.

She is wicked and needs reformation. If she's ironic enough, she stays behind. It is more the broken, than the repaired who tell of a deal made with heaven's price of admission. Appearances do tell lies. I'm looking for the truth of me. But I have lacked the courage to face me down in the places of origins. The life of a girl/woman-at-large is far more serious than what is allowed to be told.

What I feel in me is a whore. A wicked woman. I lacked the courage to become the prostitute I was meant to be. So I wonder about her instead.

Maman and I are sitting in chairs on the porch—piazza dad calls it. Dad is gone to bed. Tired from the mill, he always goes to bed early.

"I feel like a bag of chips," I tell *maman*. It is almost 8:30 and late summer. The darkness is waiting in the wings.

"Stay, home, don't go," she counters. Almost whining.

"No, I'll just take a run up to the store," I say. "I really feel like a bag of chips."

"It is getting late. I don't want you to go." she tells me.

"I'll be right back." I laugh at her.

I am physically fit. I run and ride a bike. I play soft ball with the neighborhood boys. I am sixteen. Sure of myself. Solid in my shoes and on my feet. I know the land like the back of my hand. One quick run up the street and back in time for dead darkness to settle in.

I come out of the store and instinctively I know I'm in big trouble. Parked by the curb is a car full of six teenage boys. Older boys. No one from the neighborhood. No one familiar. My blood runs cold. I hear what they are saying about me and I hear their plans. I walk with a steady step. I cannot allow them to see my fear. I open my chips and crunch them loud. One by one. Calculating what I will need to do. The streets are haunted and deserted. The doors shut up tight. Darkness came sooner as *maman* said it would. I can see how the deck is stacked. Everyone on this crowded street has taken to their nightly habit of anticipating tomorrow. Uttering undirected, incoherent wisps of prayer. Shades pulled. Doors locked.

The boys are getting braver and louder. I'm becoming a piece of ass with great rapidity. I measure the distance to home. I begin to run at a trot. Just to pick up the tempo. Let the boys worry about losing me. They are pulling in close to me on the sidewalk and I am a hunted animal. Chased and soon to be cornered. I have one advantage. I can pull a fast one, and they will have trouble from their point of laziness, not quite willing to come out of the car, yet, to get at me.

"Hey, baby, let's do it."

"Would you like a ride?"

"We've got something for you and just for you."

To themselves they say: "Get the bitch."

"Hey, whore. Come on, get in."

My mind is full of retort. But more than that, I am afraid, and I am aware of how alone with them I am. The street is so eerily empty.

I go past where I will be cutting a short cut. I run right past and they drive ahead of me and wait for me to show up to continue their personal invitations to me as synthetic streetwalker.

They sit there for a while because I don't show up. They turn around. Looking for me. Where is the bitch gone they say angrily because I have given them the slip. I am crouched behind a car in a friend's yard. Even the basketball court across the street is empty. I realize I should have listened to *maman*. Too late, now. I think. I have three ways to go home. They turned around again to go back the way they had come looking for me, only to turn around and to go ahead to wait for me once again. I take this opportunity to run really fast down the least known street and home. I realize this was the loneliest route and they would have access to me if they saw the connecting road between the one they were on and the one I was now running down. We could meet up face-to-face. And to get home, I still had to run through two fields to reach my yard.

I sink into my chair on the porch and finish my precious bag of chips which I have been clutching while running.

Maman is relieved to have me on the porch with her.

Our porch faces the road that leads to the public men's softball field. The road that the carful of boys had been on. There are games every night. Under the lights.

Driving by the house, I see the carful of the six boys. They are drinking. Loud. From the safety of my porch I want to yell out something to them, but I remain quiet. Still, I laugh to myself.

"What's so funny," *maman* wants to know.

"See that car of boys," I tell *maman*.

She looks up over her double-vision glasses.

"They just chased me, but I got away." I told her how.

"I told you to stay home," she said. "You didn't need to go get those god-damned potato chips."

"Yeah, but. I made it," I tell her while crunching the very last chip.

THE EDUCATION OF WOMEN—H.C. Dane Esq., has been lately contributing to one of our leading journals some thoughtful considerations in reference to this topic...The arguments adduced by the writer alluded to are appalling and the worst thing about it is they are true. Take the matter of dress for example:

Paris gives woman her style of dress. Paris, with its idea of female virtue: Paris, with its female license and abandonment; Paris, with its legalized system of prostitution, gives Christian America its style of female dress, which is studied for one great purpose—to fascinate the eyes and arouse the passions of men...It is plain, then, if we would remove the social evil we must first signalize its causes and remove them, not only by penal enactment but the introduction of a truer and more Christian education of the sex.

—*The Waterville Mail, Vol. XXIV, No. 23 December 2, 1870*

Chapter 34

Not Only By Penal Enactment

A parable according to Water Street:

So again, we are arguing with God. Where the hell are you? And what is the point of taking such a long coffee break? Where the hell can we find you? Strap us down with these puny needs or appetites while you go off to be cool and be God. Running the universe, you say? Why can't you do it from here or where we can see you? To keep the lobbyist off your back. So you can think more clearly? Test run for eternity, you say? A little housekeeping detail?

Jesus as Man? If you were a truly brave God, Jesus could have been Josephine. Except the first time she spoke **She** would have been crucified. At once! Pharisees were afraid of Jesus. Afraid he'd make more like him. Sent the temple whore down to check it out. 'Cept she had a foot fetish. Fell in love 'cause Jesus wasn't a bad-looking boy and he had had experience with an adulteress and sand writing. He knew who that woman had been with. Knew the man's name—was writing it in the sand. Big, local mob boss. Everybody owed him some money or was getting a cut in his deals. No one had the cash ready and they wanted their cash flow to remain lucrative so they decided to let the mob boss' woman live. Just some funky chick up from Jerusalem anyway. She was leaving town next week. No need to upset the mob boss. They began to give their excuses: Gotta go get supper! Horse needs feed. I need new shoes. My mother's calling me. I have to go pee. I've lain with her myself. Maybe Jesus will write my name in the sand next. Let's go wife. We're wasting our time. Bra strap broke. See ya. No one was left. Jesus wipes out the mob boss's name. Where did they all go? She knew about Jesus from Mary M, so she just smiled. We, adulteresses talk, too, she thinks. Jesus says: Have a nice day. Walks away. Everyone thinks he said, "Go and sin no more." But Jesus was not interested in her sins, but her saving soul. She was worth more alive than dead. Everyone who saw her would remember. Go and sin no more. So her name got to be Godisinnomore. Shortened to Goddess. Sister to Jesus.

Our BRIDGE is about ready for crossing. They have nearly completed the filling of the abutment at the east side from the sand hill above, and will immediately fill the western abutment from the same source. We ought to have a day of rejoicing when the bridge is opened for travel.

LATER.—Hurrah! The contractors have gone ahead of their promises, and the bridge, although not quite finished, is open for travel—
—*The Waterville Mail, Vol. XXIV, No. 23 December 2, 1870*

Chapter 35

Not Quite Finished, Is Open
For Travel——

There are moments when life is always a series of broken moments.

I see him chasing her across the lawn. It is four o'clock in the afternoon. Summer. He's just got home from the mill. She has on a blue stripped, sleeveless shirt. Shorts. And sensible shoes. She always wore sensible shoes around the house which were the ugliest piece of shoe leather you ever saw. For a while she had me wearing the same embarrassing type of shoes. Girl Scout shoes she'd called them. Good for your feet. But I put a stop to that. I had to go out in public and I wasn't about to be laughed at because of my shoes. *Maman* had pretty shoes to go in public. Bunny's mother made her wear even uglier shoes than I had to wear. Putting ugly shoes on your daughter's feet made her some kind of freak and left her open to ridicule by her not-so-gentle Catholic girl schoolmates. To the boys you were sexless. Ugly shoes worked better than a chastity belt. But the school classmates were the worst. Attacking one of their own. Inbred cruelty. Church-sanctioned, sponsored abuse. The reward system of affection from the nuns run by competition. Spit. You learn fast that you don't want their holy pictures. Don't need them. If you're smart. Or the choice spots while patrolling the younger kids in the playground, churchyard parking lot. Not a piece of gym equipment in sight. I would like to sneak Bunny some different shoes. She is a target of the pecking order. I was set up to be in their range, but I deftly deflected their emotional punches. By laughing at them. Not caring what they had to tell me. Rendering their peck, peck, peck to size. "Why don't you go back to the farm where you came just moved from," was how I was welcomed back to the convent after a year long hiatus. "Did you think I wanted to come here and to be with you?" I sneered back. My distaste was real. I hated them all. I hated the school and its compression. I would mark the days off the calendar when my release from the Catholic hell hole would begin. When I would be allowed to walk free in the halls of public school. Breathe in air perfumed with boys. We were all French Catholic girls in school, but we were rivals to the death for First Chair. Seated according to intelligence, I won the First Chair once and laughed my victory over the usual girl who always had First Chair. I only wanted to prove I could get it I told her. To undo its myth.

After Alcoholism, school was the first wake-up call this child had as to the condition of the world. You were tossed about on a sea of emotions. Happy childhood was a rare commodity, but you made the best of it and you improvised. And like any other situation where you are not in control of your destiny, there are the good moments that go along with the bad. It's not always abuse for supper table talk. But the world of rewards with the nuns was not a place of making merry.

He was chasing her across the lawn with a coffee cup in hand. Hot, steaming coffee.

She got to the door first and as she ran into the bedroom just off the kitchen, he not far behind, heaved the whole cup of hot coffee at her. He hit the wall and his bureau, but most importantly, she was drenched. All of her back was covered in coffee and down her arms. Coffee was spread all over the floor. And on the wall. She wailed. She swore. He walked out, vindicated of his supremacy to rule over his woman and his domain. Satisfied. He left the shit right where it hit the wall. She changed her clothes. Sad. But very, very mad. I can only watch. Be confused as to the meaning of what happens in the house called home. She forgave him. She lived with him for years and years afterwards. Everyone swears in French.

In a town not quite ready for living, living goes on. In French. Never quite prepared, always on the verge, but never really making a serious effort to understand the French on their terms. Angry at the intrusion of a foreign folk. A foreign speaking *monde*. Foreign born. Banished to the river banks. Hidden behind the curtain of shame they brought with them down the Canada Road—sorry for being poor. Humble because hungry people are always humble. Having enough to eat makes one insensitive. Haughty. Proud.

The hard-working French. Willing to pitch in, but keeping to themselves and their ways, therefore misunderstood. The environment never built to accommodate them in their manner of being. And then their women suffered under the hand of their men because of the peck, peck, peck of a ill-prepared community to meet them at their own worth. Progress its own measure and reward. Like a bridge spanning the river Kennebec, nature is tampered with to fit needs. Keep up with the pace. Women heavy with child, walking slower than the rest with two or three children by her side as well. Poor, ill-kept because the dirt is close at hand when the land is more than metaphor. Poverty of spirit in the flesh. Equality a bonus prayer. A plenary indulgence of the rewards in heaven that you can only dream about. The sidewalk I walk on leaks the blood of my *maman*'s *papa* who lay down to die when she was four. I am walking daily over his street death spot. Drunk from being intoxicated with trying to make sense of the poverty. He lay down and gave up. That's how *mémère* became a widow. Life accused him of inconsistency with the pattern of the land he was standing on and the ransom he paid was his life. Confused, by lack of association. Lack of a common language. She went on to live for decades without him. Not much had changed. The worth of the price of a human being tempered in French had not risen because the market will not bear what it cannot bear.

There are men delivering large cement round sinks the men would use to wash their hands at the mill. They have a base and a deep circular well on top of the base. They look like giant dessert dishes on a stem. Flower pots dad says. The mill was replacing them with newer models. Dad asked to buy two. The men laughed at him. "What are you going to do with those, *Côté?*" He evaded answering. He always evaded answering. He bought two for *maman*. To plant her flowers in. To plant our flowers in he said. Every year they fill the sinks with flowers they choose from his cousin the florist. He fills the sinks with dirt and they plant the flowers together and weed them every night. They make silent love to one another over the flower bed. They are at peace with each other in the flowers. She is equal to him in the planting. She won't leave him because she tells me, "She's pounded as many nails in the roof as he did," in this house they built together. She dies not wishing to speak with him. He plants flowers on her grave which he sends me for and I come back with the wrong color! I was not paying attention to the picture he was pointing to—I bought the right kind, but I must realize she had her favorite color of flowers and he was determined to put them on her grave. After he died, I planted permanent bushes besides each side of the tombstone he picked out for her—her favorite—praying hands are etched on its heart-shaped face. Everything I planted for him dies until I get it right. He wanted a cedar bush. My father talks to me through the land around his grave. When my brother died, he blew a limb off a tree and scattered its remains all around. He has the power to do this. The man who exploded all around us when he was living has the power to lay trees in ruin from his grave. He speaks to me in white pine. Some days he is gentle in pine cones.

A correspondent of the Boston Traveler says that if women were as particular in the choosing of a virtuous husband as men are in choosing a virtuous wife, a moral reformation would be soon begun.

—*The Waterville Mail, Vol. XXIV, No. 27 December 30, 1870*

Chapter 36

If Women Were As Particular In The Choosing

I seem to see a wave engulfing the place where women stay.

I am my *maman*'s only daughter. My sense of self can sometimes only know or recognize me when I remember my *maman*. My understanding of my being in the present realizes itself by looking at my past through a telescope. It begins in her face; her smiling face and I think of tanned wrinkles, or a frustrated, in-a-hurry, run-ragged woman. I experienced a comfortableness, an acceptance with curious objections that came from her. Sometimes she did not recognize me.

From that shore of *maman*, I was launched. To the shores of all others. That is why I need to think of her anchoring self. Her, as point of origin and departure. Her, as central. Each step I've taken, I take away from her. It feels as if my life is a movement away from the mother/spirit and into a life of my own.

He wrote:

Love in the sunshine
love when it rain
love best off all when
my hart is full of pain.

That is a love poem in laborer's language. Speaking on the same level as the angels do to all of us. The secrets of the universe, ours, wrapped in pain. The lessons of living falling like rain on our private gardens. As long as we have a safe harbor or a safe shelter.

Maman. All *mamans*. The mother's heartache untold is trying to get her children to listen and to follow in their right paths. The *maman* talking to you telling you to pick up your room. The burden of training and making moral humans out of our children. Without crushing them or taking away their spirit of adventure. On a mission of living your life? Take the umbrella and an extra blanket. And here's a plate of good food. Sometimes the kids will surprise you and cook a waffle in return. And put it in the oven to stay warm while the dog has an epileptic seizure. Sometimes they will break your heart of hearts and expect you to love them just the same. And *mamans* do. *Mamans* love because *mamans* love. Even when their heart is full of pain. Children love when their heart is full of pain. That's when love is best, when the heart of hearts is broken. Secret love. Love only God can feel. Love eternal because there is no reason for it existing or for going on, but it does. Even in the most hopeless of circumstances. And amidst insult and cracked ribs or blackened eyes.

You need to get yourself away from that man. Go live by yourself somewhere so he won't be able to hit or hurt you anymore.

I'm not leaving.

I'm so confused.

Why, dear God, why do I deserve this?

What did I do to deserve this?

You didn't do anything.

Why does that man hate me so bad?

I'm better than him. I'm worth something.

Don't listen to what he tells you.

Your father and I are coming for a ride.

I thought you were…

Oh, we patched things up.

Waterville, Maine
Oct 31. 1939

Dear Sweetheart

Yes I was glad to see you honey I love to see all the time. Sweetheart.

I am sorry to heare you say that had cramps all day. Gee it hard for you is it.

I am glad that you are coming to Waterville for a week honey.

I wish that you will git good luck too.

Yes I am going to see my Sweetheart for Sat. night the only that I love too. I hope that it dont rain like it's raining to day.

You are not a cry baby honey I know that I would not like to be all by myself all the time.

I love to have you by my side honey.

I am going to church tonight and tomorrow too at five o'clock. Well I'll have to close now the news are scarse in Waterville.

But is one thing I want to say to you that do love big honey and very big to. Honey do miss you very much. I do think of you in the day time too. Well good night so long honey.

With all my love
Ray.

I LOVE
   YOU
      big

THE MEEK SHALL INHERIT THE EARTH.—

The mild races in the long run are the most powerful. I think the strangest text in the Bible, if you interpret it from the face of things, is this: "Blessed are the meek for they shall inherit the earth." If it had been, "Blessed are the meek; for they shall inherit something better than the earth," it would not have been so strange: but to say that the meek shall *inherit the earth* is to [sic] much. --

H.W. Beecher

—*The Waterville Mail, Vol. XXIV, No. 25 December 16, 1870*

Chapter 37

It Would Not Have Been So Strange

The song is not done until it is finished or the story is not complete of itself. She is not worried about taking up time because the song/story would not be complete if she worried about taking up time. She needs to bring the song/story to completion. She always says thank you immediately for our listening to her as well as her name. She says she tires of her own singing. She realizes that she is her own audience, first and foremost. She says she sings everywhere at all times. This is her work.

I am waiting to hear her sing. To me. The music strikes a chord of reason in my being. It gives me understanding which I can get no place else. The heart knows its song by itself—heart. Because the rhythm is identical and in tune. Musical tune. Other songs are discord. But a heartsong is descant and harmony. Point and counterpoint. I had no idea what I was waiting to hear when I heard her sing for the first time. She opened her mouth and I knew. Her work she calls it.

It is in this stepping away from *maman* which reminds me acutely of my solitude, solitariness. Not known because my points of reference to my being is dead—*maman* is dead; unexplained because the one who bore me and knew my heart carried that away with her. She is afloat in her own new self-definition.

To be known as I exist is a luxury. To be known deeply and understood without any unnecessary words of explanation is prayer. Prayer of recognition. Prayer of rejoicing.

I have a friend who has been my friend for many years. Bunny. She knows me. She is a woman who can explain or know or recognize the meaning of my being. I can attest to her and her life. Daily we meet new people. Sometimes the new people are our own children. I could never attest for all of *maman*'s life like she could for me—only the parts I knew. The older we become, the more difficult it is to explain ourselves unless there are those who can attest for us.

I cannot explain myself very well. I cannot easily lay down the patterns, templates, threads, needles, scissors, sewing machines which fabricated my life. I can try, but without points of reference, even I get lost in the explaining.

Why do I do the things I do or how I do them? Where does that gesture originate? Where do my expressions or language come from? I have a nervous habit the same as *maman*'s, where did she get it?

In isolation we lack definition. For some this is not the case, but to live as if unexplained, or in a kind of isolation from family or community is a cruelty developed by modern society. Even though people close to me have died, I go on, but I view it as dangerous business and bravery.

The woman sings another traditional, French-Canadian folk song, my music, and I feel explained.

THE SINGER'S SEWING MACHINE PATENT.

    —One of the Singer sewing-machine patents expires next Friday, and the refusal to extend it is officially announced to-day…as there are a number of other patents having several years to run, which protect the Singer Manufacturing Company…several of the existing patents do not expire untill [sic] 1877…

                     —*The Waterville Mail, Vol. XXIV, No. 22 November 25, 1870*

Chapter 38

Having Several Years To Run

There is a coming home that has nothing in common with our present day life. We all do it. We go home. Somehow or other we go home. We encounter our sacred. Our secrets and our self. Once you have made the journey away from the self, you return, to who you are. Our entire life is a story of coming home. Spiritually, we arrive *chez-nous* through nuances. But the joy of living in the present is to go as far back as I can and to really pick up the scent of the responses which the ancestors gave. Because, here I stand, and there they were, in their meanings, just as real. Family counts. Despite the feuds. We who have a reason for belonging.

The small town in France that my husband and I visited from which our mutual relatives of the 1600s emigrated is called *Tourouvre*. My husband and I are ninth and tenth cousins. In the Franco-American constellation husbands and wives are often cousins. Sometimes first cousins. Sanctioned by the church. As one man in Louisiana told me about his marrying his first cousin—"we're thoroughbreds." Love knows no boundaries, no artificial rules, and it breaks them as often as it can. Falling in love with a place is coming home. Centuries after the ancestors left, I walk back into the town and it is like the place has been waiting for me all these years to come home. It's like a lover that steals into your room one night when you never expected such a honor would be bestowed. For those who left, it is a parting which never heals. That's why I came back, the love wound given needed to be healed and laid to rest. I went home for those who left 400 years before. Through my eyes, looking at the past which was the present, I understood myself. What I saw resembled the feeling of having been there before, but in this case I knew I had been there through the ancestors and their memories in me. The Garden of Eden of our consciously knowing home has many doors.

It equates with having a story to tell. Over and over again. Knowing the ancestral lines is a road map back home. The leaves on the tree point to the directions of the roots. The river's mouth is but the accumulation of the streams' flow. We crossed the ferry from Dover, England into France. *Calais*. Calay. Calais in Maine. Calass. Pronounced differently in New France. I had been to England before. I like England well enough on my first visit, but if I knew only one country, I could not know what I am missing. In learning France better as my homeland, I learned me. I made sense to myself. New England held very little by way of explanation of the French, or of me, as part of that heritage. I had been wandering for several generations as a woman without a country. Unexplained by the landscape. Foreign on my birth soil. Before I had left for France, I had read a book about whether or not there was a French national character. I imagined what my ancestral women thought when their last sight of their homeland was the coastline growing smaller and smaller until it disappeared entirely. Sitting on the ferry crossing the English Channel, it seemed appropriate that I should approach France by water, and that my first sights would be of its coastlines. The beaches of the coastline of France kept in longing memory so that I would be capable of carrying the honor home. The message that all was well. Sort of. We'd been captured and some of us had let go of the hope of carrying on the France of ourselves. Search and rescue never showed up so we learned to become *comme les moudgits l'anglais*. Some of us even learned the conqueror's tongue as well as our own. And some let the French language drop all together. The heart carries the message just the same. Like wayward beggars looking for a reason to be, we wandered upon ourselves almost by accident. The only real map we had was the genealogies of myself and my husband. The rest of the journey was written on the window panes of the stained glass windows of the church in *Tourouvre*. The names of the families that had left there four centuries before were spelled out like a memorial and no one seemed surprise to see us coming back four hundred years later. The *Gagnon's* had a sign pointing out the original *ferme*. *Mémère Daigle* had been right. Some of our family did come from France. Ten miles down the road, at a local restaurant and bar where we order a glass of wine and local beer, I ask if there were any *Giroux* still in the area. The woman asked me when our people had left. Sheepishly, I tell her *"quatre cent l'années,"*—four hundred years— she never blinked an eye. She gave me directions to the still-standing farm of *Toussaint Giroux* and the present-day relations. "Go there," she tells me in French, "your family is there." They continue their arguing in the kitchen. Arguing that I recognize.

In *Tourouvre* there is a museum, *Musée de l'Histoire de L'Émigration Percheronne au Canada*, which houses publications of the stories of the more than 200 individuals who left *Perche* for New France. *Perche* is no longer a *département*, county or state equivalent, in France. Ours was not only a wine tasting tour of the French countryside, our thirst ran deeper than something in which the body delighted. I could go home with the knowledge that the pilgrims intended to evangelize the New World in its ways. I had the means to run my "machine" for a few more years.

A man who was lost on the Plains, and who had lived several weeks on raw fish, desiring to vary his bill of fare, says he pursued a toad for two days, but without success.

—*TheWaterville Mail,Vol. XXIV, No. 26 December 23, 1870*

Chapter 39

Lost On The Plains

The language I live in shapes my thoughts that wrap around life—its objects, places, people—and consequently shapes me. Language gives me my price of entry into my culture. Whether or not I have access to my language is a debate that leaves me longing more for words than for water. As I crossed the English Channel, I told my husband it will seem very strange to be in a place where I am *supposed* to speak French. All my life I had suppressed that language in order to live in a place where English expected to be worshipped, and French, well, French was something you lost just as soon as you took up with the *des Yankées*. Some did lose everything French. Some took up with the *des Améritchains* and changed their names in order to hide their true identity. In our original migration away from France, we headed West toward some cultural death—language maintenance almost an impossibility, but not entirely—The *Québec* of our life a northern comfort. Heading south to New England we were again at odds with ourselves. Stories abound of how the French came to populate the mills. The male and female of ourselves—English and French embodied in one person by historical association through a shared geography—at once in love with our French selves, the new French born on foreign soils, foreign nationalist forever exiled, self-exiled. There is love of my French self, but I cannot partake of it because I was not allowed a full expression of loving myself and living French in public without public shame. We are not residents on a continent of peace in our southern selves. Minding our P's and Q's for the French of New England meant *P.Q., Canada.*

On my second trip to France, I sat next to a man who had made expeditions to the North Pole, Antarctica and elsewhere. Antarctica is the only continent where war has not been waged. I have a war which I wage inside of me, and because I am at cultural war with myself, I cannot reside in peace in a place of being. Once having left we cannot go back to France. We can visit, gaze on it with wonder, admire its beauty, be shell-shocked about who we are, but we made our home in the New World and New World dwellers we are. France—a whole nation which resembles us, a sensibility not lost or misplaced, but lived as unselfconsciously as the English. And yet, conquered as I have been, or forgotten by France, I am English, too? I wish at times I could be in France where my sense of self is the same as place. My son wants to move to *Québec* for the same reason. He feels his passion and the land unite. Reclaiming French soil for one's own sanity and purpose. If we don't have the language, we certainly do have the heritage and the bloodline. One thing none of us can deny, and that is our ancestors. When I am in France it makes me so happy to be there, but also so sad that I want to cry.

Directionally speaking, I am used to facing other places than where the sun rises and sets, although for my father "headin' West" meant you became a cemetery dweller permanently, instead of simply being lost and wandering who you were and how you fit into the American plan 'down the Plains.' My father's lonesome pine was in the westerly direction where the cemetery was located. Where his ancestors are. Heading East for him meant he was going to bed—toward a comfort zone. That was how he said goodnight: "I'm headin' East." "Good night, dad," I'd reply. So to head East to France, or to come back home West is how I feel that I am in a sling-shot somewhere between life and death.

France. I just saw it written on the side of a building. It gave me a thrill. Like I own it. Or it was mine. I suppose it is on some levels. Who would guess that you would go to France and meet yourself. But I guess that is what happened. It is like dipping your finger in a well. A fountain of youth. I think now when I look into certain eyes all I see is knowing and not a question. Tensions released. Keep the box closed, I hear. I already said: no apologies allowed. Not after someone or something has just released you from some kind of prison. One devised by outside circumstances which have dragged on for years. It is attainable on some levels—this you of you. If someone or something has the key. The skeleton key which unlocks the secret passage ways among all of us. It's a matter of learning yourself and others as well. Some as lovers. Some as hags. Some as weepers. Freshly divorced or married. Leg touching leg; arm brushing arm and the constant sound of a "no" coming from the zephyr's twin. I cannot be faulted for my life. Its path and mine have run concurrently. I cannot be faulted historically for leaving France, *Québec* to come to live in a land of foreign tongues—English is a foreign tongue— language. Living in English is only partially the truth. Living in French is to hold onto a promise. Is it a promise or more like an invitation? To belong. It has more to do with what I most long for and cannot always have. There are dreams and there are hopes. I can only belong or believe in one at a time. The unholy and the holy in the same place.

I sit myself in a low place and I am surrounded by the heap—somewhere the unlikely places I find myself surrounded by reasons why and why not French. The message is given and I am cut off. There is a surprise in that box. It is more like a chance to display brilliance. To express thought. It is how it comes to mind. They press bodies; souls collide. In truth and in consequence. The phone rings back home. I am going to Paris today.

In three hours and a half Thursday forenoon 115 teams passed the new bridge...Our streets are presenting signs of life unknown for years past, when we had only a toll bridge...It yet remains to be seen that the citizens of Waterville have not even yet fully opened their eyes to a just estimate of what has been accomplished for their prosperity, by Winslow, in making their bridge free...

—*The Waterville Mail, Vol. XXIV, No. 26 December 23, 1870*

Chapter 40

In Making Their Bridge Free

I find myself in a mood that blows like a weather vane. North, no; South, yes. I live in the United States, New England, Maine. So this time the South really wins, but coming from there I go East toward Western France. France says with her eyes that my innocence is in her. She swallowed it and I am glad. My last burden was laid upon her.

I find the evening and the company clever or at least there's the Eiffel Tower. I'm under it in a late daytime sun. The view is magnificent. I see a star and wish for a real lover like the one I forgot to pack. Love of self. My thoughts have to do with some kind of terminal sadness. Of remembering without memory. The country France went onto its own history without us émigrés. I cannot fit into a culture which does not recognize his or her own. I am back at my hotel, sitting on the balcony outside of my room. No one is sitting outside but me. I wonder why I am so drawn to this balcony when the action is on the street. In France, I find myself in a funny position. I am sure that the moment of craziness, freedom is not what I need to explain. I am my own source of re-dress. The person I know is only me.

When I was a girl, as if I am not always a girl, I never thought I'd be sitting on a balcony in Paris. It was just a strange and foreign place. *Mémère Daigle* used to say: "I think some of our relatives came from Paris, France." *Maman* always wanted to come here. So I took up some dirt under the Eiffel Tower so I could spread it on her grave when I got home. I took dirt from a French farmer's country field for my father because of his longing for the original soil was to always have a farm. With farm dirt from France spread all over his tomb maybe then the restlessness in him could come to a place of contentment. My going back to France runs generations deep in freeing the longings.

I thought or believed the lies that in France I would never find sympathy for my French. I'm on the balcony on the 5ième *étage* and I am in the air with the birds and the view of the half moon unclouded. I've found the East and so I know the West. I'm not sure of the direction of North and South. Women do not wear nylons in Paris. I see them wearing some clunky shoes.

Traveling undoes your universe back home. I find myself challenged about who and what I am. I am explained. Me being French in Maine is explained.

This is no accident. There is a reason for me being who I am. Traveling, I am limited to one suitcase's expression of my wardrobe plus all of my inconsistencies. Which includes fat and scars. I attempt an expression of who I am in Paris. Mostly the language I speak is my appearance. There is a varying degree of elasticity. Refinement of elements such as white sugar or white flour removes the germ of personality. The manners that I have acquired become a signature of who I am and what I am capable of accomplishing in French. Including what gels into a fine paste of possibilities. My way of being on the everyday scale waits for me at home when I am through walking a tightrope in France. I will be changed.

In my Parisianistic meanderings and musings in and among known-to-me-strangers I wonder about my floating in a city of millions where there are many, many ways of being. Languages by the bucketful. And embarrassed silences. Talk flames the air between us with meaning and story. I also long to return to the comfort of my life, to the knowns, and to the English. Soon, I would give up wearing nylons if I stayed here because I would have a desire to fit in. I look around and I notice that there are trees on the rooftops. I miss my life among this unknown.

I wonder how others who live here interpret this city. Is it that time and its constraints tell us our path in life? Or is it a palette from which we draw life's colors? It's *La Femme Naturelle* here. Women not afraid of their legs. But the expression is more habit to them, therefore they cannot know their effect. It is how we come together to heal after the world surrounds us that ensures the continuation of our concurrent universes.

A porch is a balcony evolved. *Chez-nous, Québec* and *États-Unis* we sit on our porches. It is an expression of living in public, privately. Paris, I see, is full of porch living, café sitting, private in public doings. The biggest part of the ritual is to be seen. And to see, but mostly to be seen. On the balcony of our room, I sit here and I am seen. Not private as when hidden by walls and doors, but private lived as public. I wouldn't dress out here, yet somehow my presence challenges the routines below because this is a hotel and by Friday the balcony will belong to someone else, and the view will be re-interpreted, but for now, I am an émigré come home by a bridge built through the four-hundred years of exile, and I can speak French with the ones who chose to stay behind.

I went home and spread the dirt on *maman*'s and dad's grave. Wrote poems about it and won a poetry contest with the poems. I read them and played a tape of *maman*'s and dad's voices singing that I had taped when they had come to visit us when we lived in Aroostook County and the kids were little.

West Waterville Items—Mr. Jos. Blaisdell is to build a double tenement house on Water Street.

—*The Waterville Mail, Vol. XXIV, No. 27 August 8, 1870*

Chapter 41

A Double Tenement

Immigrants usually converge in neighborhoods when they come to a new country. Water Street is where the French immigrants from Canada congregated in Waterville. They were without a priest when they first came so some of them converted to the Baptist religion and their church was called the French Baptist Church. It was a sin to go into that building we were told and you would go to hell if you did. So I watched all those French people go into that building on Sunday as I walked to the"superior" Catholic church up the street and I felt sorry for all those damned-to-hell souls. How could anyone be so brave and defy the pope? The infallible pope. The man who never makes a mistake. I was impressed.

I attended a Baptist church for a time when I was a young, married woman. The man, priest who was saying mass at the Catholic church would chew the prayers so bad that I knew he had missed his true calling as an auctioneer. So I left his blasphemy and joined in with the damned. The minister impressed the young woman I was until he was the dish that ran away with the spoon, a choir member. But before all that, through his jealousy of another Protestant church in the town getting enough funds to build their own school, he pressed the congregation for money, money, money. We had none and the guilt of my poverty forced me to remain home. Years later, I found out about his escapades with women in the church. At church, progressive suppers, he always wanted a fine looking woman to be seated to his right. It felt like an honor, but one would do well to not accept invitations from wolfish ministers to sit by them for supper especially when she's pregnant. So I went back to the Catholic Church to gain access to community. Sometimes organized religion is like getting enmeshed in chicken wire. But I don't know where else ritual exists on the level that it does in the performance of the mass.

Languishing in our private lives, we come together in the sepulcher of the church to pray in unison. Years and years of ritual with a few changes due to Vatican II. Some used it as an excuse to leave. Too much change to the centuries' old false front. The feeling is that ever since Jesus walked on the earth and told Peter to build his church, things have not changed. Most Catholics have never read the Bible. So the church hierarchy is safe. Sometimes I'm afraid to go on alone in my life. Sometimes the length of the day seems like an eternity when I am the one responsible to fill it. Going to church is like visiting the grave-yard for me. It centers my point of view. Mostly, I can feel *maman* in church, and that is where or how I celebrate the anniversary of her death. I celebrate the anniversary of dad's death, too. But she was more in love with the church. She also hated the church. She loved God. Religion was her sanity. Although *maman* never saw herself as one of the church's "Litttle Big Deals." Little Big Deals were the ones who elevated their faith in a public manner. And cheated during election times at the voting booths. That would send her howling to me in a letter. For a French woman living in a small city like Waterville, church on Sunday was her stage. Getting ready for church was quite an affair. Tied down with kids and a jealous husband, she was still crazy about clothes, she would use the Sunday mass as a place to perfect her definition. She sewed beautifully. She sewed as a means of survival. She sewed in glory to God. She sewed in prayer and thanksgiving. Everyone knew it and they conceded: She had a gift. Her sewing was a blessing from the Almighty. She was a woman of the Bible with her purple sashes and linens. She didn't sew for profit until she worked at the shirt factory or in the tailor shop of a fine men's clothing store. She was one with God when she sewed. She performed perfection with the needle and thread. At the shirt factory, one of her jobs was final inspection. How she suffered. She was caught between her own sense of excellence, the mill's need for quality and the workers, her comrades, to whom she was in charge of playing shirt god. She was their judge in the life of a shirt and its maker—goats and sheep—did the shirt go on to be retailed or back upstairs to cut into the woman's averages? A returned shirt meant the woman had to rip the shirt apart in order to fix the imperfection. Sometimes she had to punch out and other times she did not lose time on her averages—these women give the dirty dozen a new meaning. These were women with a purpose on a mean sewing machine. Have you ever really looked at a man's shirt? Have you seen the pocket stripes match the shirt perfectly? I've seen maple leaves with more flaws. The man with the patch over his eye. Mr. Hathaway. He's the one who lines up the stripes for the women to sew them on. Or so the legend in my house goes. *Maman* couldn't stay on final inspection because she couldn't stand the hate coming at her for what she did so naturally—expect the best. She would come home after a day of standing and inspecting shirt after shirt—samples from bundles taken at random—and slam her pressure cooker around as well as the turnip and carrots and talk about how she took abuse from the women who got angry at her because she returned shirts. Loss of income in a piece-rate factory meant that much less food on the table for these women and their families. *Maman* did not like being in charge of that much God-work. So she quit. But she took her final inspection scissors home with her. She used them to rip things apart for the rest of her sewing life. This god wore double-vision glasses, sat on her end of the couch evenings, sewed by hand to be near him because he liked her to sit with him at night to watch TV together when he wasn't drunk and he was never drunk during the week. He had strict rules. He never missed a day of work in his life because of a hangover. No drinking during the week. She would peek over her glasses at interesting tidbits on the TV, and sew to her heart's content. Even he admired her gift. Even he had to admit that she was exceptional when it came to working magic with the cloth. Cooperating with God—that's how you get to be God, too. So, too, like God, she had a reputation to maintain. So where else would she wear her God-creations, but to His house? To pray in fashion.

Burglary—The house of Mr. Peter DeRocher, on Summer Street, was entered on Sunday night last, through the window of the sewing room…and a large amount of clothing and other articles taken out. The thief or thieves must have been frightened away in a hurry however, for the most of the articles were found strown about the yard and hidden under the fence…The thieves were evidently novices in the business for with many valuable articles, they picked up many things comparatively worthless, such as clothes pins. In their hurry and fright, the thieves left behind them articles not taken from Mr. DeRocher—a box stolen from a house on the Plain, and a coat, the pockets of which were full of stolen property…

—*The Waterville Mail, Vol. XXIV, No. 21 November 18, 1870*

Chapter 42

Such As Clothes Pins

Waiting on shore at camp for the fisherman to get back. Waiting for the drone of the engine. The familiar engine. Six horsepower Johnson motor. Way after dark and she turns on a light for him so he can find the wharf, but I don't think he needs it. She does it as a courtesy so he can find her. This is an old and wise man. Once, while working the yard and the log drive at the pulp and paper mill, a man fell into the Kennebec. Dad jumped in to pull him out of the river. He had to dive many times to bring him up. Dad always used to swim in the Kennebec when he was a boy. He knew the currents. He told me, "When you swim in a river, don't try to fight the current. Don't go against the current, or you'll get tired and go under. Swim across the current and you'll get where you need to go." How many times in your life will you need to know how to swim in a river? Well, one time I went canoeing and both of the canoeists were inexperienced. Five times we capsized and five times I swam across the river's current. This river trip was a lot like living. Learning to swim across the current.

The river trip also reminded me of pregnancy. Once begun, you have to finish the trip. I came out of that river like I came out of my three pregnancies; I knew myself much better than when I went in. And I have premonitions. All the women in my family do. I had a vision of the rope wrapping itself around my ankle above my sneaker, and the canoe dragging me downriver unable to get the rope off my leg. I was pulled under. So, I canoed bare foot. The boat capsized in the freshet and the rope wrapped itself around my ankle and I slipped it off. But first I looked back at my canoeing companion and very calmly said to him, "The rope is wrapped around my leg." I was very foolish and became angry at the river, the canoe and I dragged my feet on bottom. We were in a party of many canoeists and I did not want to be further humiliated by needing their help to retrieve our canoe. I held the canoe by the rope and told my companion to come get me and the canoe. He ran on water. Just like Jesus. He had no doubts like Peter, so he never sank. We got back into our boat; I had nightmares about ropes and water and canoes that night. I took to waiting on shore. Until we got a bigger boat. And if they go night fishing, I take my turn guiding them home like the beacon the women of our family can be.

Maman like to build fires at camp. "Pyro," we called her.

"I'm going to make a little fire," she'd say, "just to get rid of some of these leaves."

And she'd burn all day. Face hot. Ritual. It became a ritual. Fire start-ing. Burning. Out of the excuse of necessity. To clean up the leaves at camp which was built in a hill. It took three sets of stairs to climb back up to the road. She did not want to haul the leaves out so she burned them. But it got to be an obsession. The eternal flame. Before the days of clean air acts. At home, we burned our trash in a rusted-out barrel. I would carry the kitchen trash out to the barrel each day, throw in a match and walk away. I would throw in aerosol cans for a thrill. I would sit on the porch and wait for the explosion. Satisfaction, I felt satisfaction at the kaboom! Planes overhead would break the sound barrier. The mill would relieve itself through the steam valves. *Maman* would burn and burn those leaves. She couldn't swim so her baptism had to be by fire, she couldn't get it any other way. Not until she was 58 years old did she learn to swim. And then she framed her certificate. To expunge Romeo's, her eleven year-old brother's drowning who fell through the ice riding atop a load of logs. The past no longer held her prisoner. The water as enemy disappeared. Like a child, she'd tell me to watch her swim. I keep the frame in an honorable place. The fire often smoldered all night and come morning she would begin all over again. Leaves as sacrificial lambs.

THE CATHOLICS, as we learn, have purchased of Mr. John Ware the old Sanger homestead on which to erect a church. After a large outlay they have concluded to abandon their enterprise on the Plains, though it must involve quite a loss.

—*The Waterville Mail, Vol. XXV, No. 23 July 14, 1871*

Chapter 43

Their Enterprise On The Plains

Teeming life and ghosts go hand-in-hand. I am both. I am at once the quick and the dead. I have tasted both and they are equal. Sometimes you can't walk for the congestion from all the ghosts. Those who have been there before you and go on to parallel universes. Doing commerce, horse trading, making love, stealing, looking you right in the eye and fortune telling. From the past. Fortunes are messages from the past. My fate is penciled in. Eternity waits. And it can go to hell for all I care. She did not want to marry a farmer. Why, I ask myself, did a *St. Germain* which, she was, and for which *boulevards, fôrets,* churches, *cafés* and more are named in France, did she resent marrying a man she considered a farmer? Was it just because she wanted to leave all that behind her when she left Wallagrass in the St. John River Valley in Northern Maine back during those late Depression years? Her mother had remarried, a man who did not believe in education for women. They fought about *mémère*'s daughters who were in school, and his grown girls who were not even contemplating education. *Mémère* who had worked in the mills in Fall River when she was ten years old knew the value of an education for her daughters. *Mémère* had a plan for *maman*. That's what *maman* told me. She was supposed to be a school teacher and help take care of her *maman* in her later years as payment for the care she received as a girl. *Maman* moved to Bangor when she had just turned seventeen to be a nanny and then to work at the Eastern Maine General Hospital. *Maman* quit school in her sophomore year. She was introduced to Ray in front of Notre Dame Church. "I didn't like him in the beginning," she said. "He was cocky and a wise guy." I think she was in denial. I think he turned her on. My brother caught her dancing on the table for dad one night. He teased her through the years that she was dancing naked. She was indignant in her denial—till later. "I was in my bra and panties!" she laughed, admitting to her lustiness she lived with her husband. The 40's and 50's notion of living the high sex life. Dancing on the table. Must be some kind of ancient ritual transformed to modernity. Belly dancing without the veils. Who could afford veils anyway? Veils was for nuns, not for table dancers like *maman*.

They would fight about property. All of them. Land. Who owned the land. Between husband and wife. My husband who is my cousin, ninth or tenth, will give me a look and I ask him, "How old is that look?" Our ancestors left France on the same boat 400 years ago. *Jean Côté*, the patriarch, cannot be exactly traced to a specific town in France, but he is buried on the *I'le Orléans* in *Québec*. *Pépère Côté* always threatened his wife, Annie, with homelessness. She was a *Giroux* whose people lived not even ten miles from the town which *Jean Côté* is reputed to have emigrated from. *Maman* married a farmer. She did everything she said she wouldn't do. I figure the sex must have been good. After the fights they had, I can imagine the make-up matched its intensity and ferocity. Otherwise, why keep doing it? Until they both got old and tired. But love, love like theirs, is addictive. Some people love in kindness and others love in violence. Ferocity. She wasn't the kind of woman to understand a tame man. In her secret self, she wanted to be man-handled and she got more than she bargained for. And the times encouraged the he-man to be he-men. Abusive relationships—the depravity of proving your manhood through brute strength and their women who insist they do—until it is too late for many. She fell in love with him and that was her fate. Her past telling her her future. He was always in her life. When she had moved to Water Street with her family as a little girl and he was a little boy, he knew her then. One Christmas, as a joke, he put a red light in the socket over the door. He always decorated the house outlined in lights, but that year he added an extra touch in the socket above the door. She was innocent of the meaning of the joke. My brother told on him. She took the broom and broke the bulb in the socket. Christmas reminds me of the red light districts.

He had always been street wise. She, a child of the light. He, a son of darkness with a skin tone to match if he stayed in the sun. She was a blond and he was dark-haired with very little gray and high cheek bones and the cunning of a fox.

They built the house together. He installed an extra long tub. Before they moved in, he carried buckets and buckets of water to fill the tub for her so she could soak. Like a true lover, he sometimes was.

Gardens and flowers and age old animosities. Those were the things of their enterprise down the Plains.

Encore Une Catastrophe

    Le train à grande vitesse qui partit de Boston à 1 hr.p.m., lundi, a été jeté hors de la voie sur le pont qui traverse la rivière Merrimack, près de Haverhill, Mass. Neuf passagers ont été lancés dans l'éternité et près de 30 personnes ont reçu des blessures plus ou moins grandes

           —L'Indépendant, 4ième année, No. 2 Foi, loyauté, progrès, Fall River, Mass, 13 janvier, 1888

Chapter 44

Ont Été Lancés dans l'Éternité

Just yesterday I moved toward my past. I could not help but remember it is the scars that we return to on anniversary days. Or nights. My father's anger and my sexuality converge at a point of intersection. I am explained in his anger's memory. Birthdays and balloons. It is through the pains of living we are provided with the turnstile of learning to enter the plains of knowing.

We are on our way to Portland for a weekend. It is my father's birthday once again. I look at a photo of him when he was ten or so and I see a thirty-year old midget. Serious and somber. The cares of his life foreknowledge. This little boy never had a balloon to play with. He was too burdened by cares in his childhood to take on the weight of a balloon. I can see that in his face in the photo. He is eighty earth years; spiritually, he entered eternity twelve years previous. On the highway, I make my plans. I will buy him a Happy Birthday balloon and tie it to the bush besides the headstone in the cemetery underneath the lonesome pine. I think of where there is a florist shop and I remember one on Water Street.

In 1969, I was companion to the drunk. The "drunk from Water Street" my boyfriend had told me. We stand at the corner of Water and Gold Streets, he and I, boyfriend and girlfriend. I am crying. I cannot tell him why he cannot walk me home. I don't want to tell him. He is persistent. Finally, I say, "because, my father may be drunk." "Is that all," he says. He laughs. "My father is drunk all the time." He kisses me and walks away. I was afraid to lose my new boyfriend because I lived with an alcoholic. Well, he lived with an alcoholic too. So we had something in common. We could tell each other about the Friday or Saturday night fights. The drunk songs that played all night long. The Singing Nun serenading the *soûlard*.

During that summer of '69, I fished and did carpentry work. I was to be his sobriety. If things were to get rough or if dad was too ugly, I was told to walk a mile down the camp road and go call *maman* at work and she would come and get me. Those were the conditions of my sixteenth summer which I shared with my father. At the same time, there were rules of propriety governing my sexuality, such as you can't date any boys until you are sixteen. Well, when I was sixteen, I did not have a boyfriend. We lived a dichotomy of existence.

I wonder about the work detail program of keeping my father sober. I wonder if it was also a program to protect my unchallenged virginity? These were strict, old-fashioned, French, Catholic people brought up in the thick of living earlier in the century, illegitimate children and shame as dinner table companions. The supper hour in hell with alcoholism as the honored guest as well as French, Catholic, Water Street girls fresh into their virginity unplucked. The vilification of the open season on cardboard cut-out whores was the running favorite opinion. Those made-up boasts by visitors to the district. A town of art museums at an "ivy" league college and dead nuns running close second to each other vying for headlines. Shame of belonging to the culture blasted in newsprint. Deep, entrenched madness of one representing the unfit nature of all. Accused. Subliminally, unacquitable, all of them, perpetrator and victim. Nothing of any worth here. Leave them all to go to eternal, living hell. These are the memories, re-born continually, in an unexamined way of life in an entire community. Who are these French people living in this town's race-horse quality bet to reach the finish line of upper crust living?

He fished. I painted. I had discovered the miracle of burying heartache in oil based artist's paints and canvas boards. I was innocent of stretched canvases. I only knew virginity as stiff and unnatural canvas boards. I had not the luxury of experiencing without guilt, the loveliness or richness of stretched canvases. That was not to be for my kind. I committed sin by entering the art supply store. My spirit of French woman proclaimed in my step and manner, "Unclean!" I bought and paid for the stolen gratification of creating beauty in defiance of the hatefulness and ugliness I was assigned to belong to as a member of my family and culture. I painted the undersoul of the alcoholic and his wife and their children. I defied the elements of the geography we stood on with a tear-off paper palette, oils, linseed oil, turpentine, expensive and sinful brushes and canvas board. I sinned luxuriousness of spewed color. I recorded a sunset for my father. We sat in the boat and I marveled at the sunset. The magic of the lake unparalleled in its beauty. Some geography more favored by God's touch than others. He told me he'd never noticed a sunset before.

"What do you mean you've never noticed the sunset before? You've been coming to Great Pond for years and years. It's right there. How could you miss it?"

"*J'l'ai jamais vu,*" he insisted. "*Moudgit pas fin.*" He liked to call himself names. Goddamned without sense.

"I cannot believe you never saw the sunset," I insist from the veil of my sixteen years. Fresh childhood not yet wiped from my eyes.

"I never saw the sunset," he tells me emphatically "until you pointed it out to me."

I am completely incredulous. I think he's lying. I find him sitting in the Aidirondack chair, one of a pair, like two swans mated for life sitting in the front of the camp, facing the sunset. My father is sitting down. He's not working, sucking in his coffee and sitting—doing nothing, but staring at the sun in his intense French way of observing the world around him. From his observations he would make pronouncements. At home, he would always sit for twenty minutes or so in his chair when he came home from the mill, drink his 3:30 PM, three-minutes-on-the-boil coffee, tell my mother stories *du polpe mill*, but she was nowhere in sight, at the tailor shop, sweltering, remaking men's suits. He was on vacation from his 36 years of accumulated time at the mill. What was my father doing sitting?

"What are you doing?" I accuse him, guilty of sitting, doing nothing, in my tone of voice.

"I'm watching the sunset, *moudgit pas fin*," he tells me in his new knowledge. Whenever my father was into self-knowledge, he always discredited any previous knowledges. He was always goddamned without sense.

I am suspicious.

"Why are *you*," still accusing tone, "watching the sunset?"

"All these years I come here to camp," he pronounces, "and I never once ever took the time to notice the sunset until you pointed it out to me the other day." I feel puffed up and proud in my sixteen year old self. Aged beyond my years. Embarrassed, because now I know he means what he said, and that he really had been depriving himself of sunsets for years and years. We go out into the boat to fish. He'd bought me my own license since I was old enough to need one. The game warden shows up. Checks our licenses. We are fishing in front of the camp. My father became respectful to the game warden like he was when the priest came to visit once a year to collect a donation. He assumes his role of small, common man among the order of things. My *maman* and I know better come Friday night and his drinking. We are the small and inconsequential. After the game warden leaves, the embarrassment still fresh in my father's face, guilty of sins not showing on the surface, he tells me like he's beyond amazement and glad he's an upstanding citizen and purchased fishing licenses for both of us: "I've never been stopped by a game warden before on this lake." I'm upsetting his comfortable universe I can see. And, he tells me. "It must be you," he says. Of course, who else could he blame?

I sit at home on the lawn of Water Street and I paint outdoors. Everytime I paint, I paint outdoors. I don't know anything about oil painting. I just stand in front of the counter of the rows and row of oil paints in the very classy stationary and gift store, my idea of American elegance in the home decorating tastes displayed in contrast to the Franco-American decor of imitation Hummels. Family photos. Doilies. Statues. Three-foot Jesus on the cross with the giant rosary beads over the headboard of my parent's bed. Who could have sex in that atmosphere? My *maman*'s *avant garde* forays into the Top Value Stamp elegance of a man praying over his daily bread. Her *Temple Stuart* dining room set. Hard-rock maple with two captains chairs, which created a huge discussion of Captain and Co-Captain in the house. She was no Co-captain, that's for sure. So, I enter the world of the artist supplies and earn my money to learn how to paint because I'm going to be an interior decorator. I have fantasies of what an artist is supposed to do. Where did I get these notions? On TV? From books. Old movies. The fantasies constrict my movements and create guilt much bigger than the taboo of an unworthy purchasing holy art supplies. Still, I sin in my movements of creating art in my own way without anyone's permission. I set up TV trays outside, plastic ones, to hold my supplies. I have a small, tabletop easel, metal; an artist's box suitcase, stained, to hold my paints and brushes. I own linseed oil because a clerk passing by answered my question impatiently about the use of it. I sparingly add drops to my larger tube of white. I'm sinning in oil paints under the Silver Maple tree. Alone. I paint the sunset from memory. All day I create a landscape not true to the real geography, but one in my mind of land mirroring the water. The water is non-reflective and the land echoes unevenly the shape of the water. I run a horizon line in a color of nonsense. The painting is light and daytime. Too bright to register the end of itself, so I mix black with all the colors and swirl the night into the canvas board. It begins to rain toward the end of my day. *Maman* and dad help me to carry my TV trays, paints, easel, canvas board, pots of turpentine, paper palette into the kitchen. She is getting supper. I am in the doorway, in the traffic pattern, in everybody's way and they never say a word to me of complaint. They go around me and let me paint by the aluminum screen door as the rain gently falls on the porch without a roof.

In order for him to finish off the inside of the camp modeled on the room he had seen at the Bangor House in old time Bangor, she and he had gone to some farm to get authentic barn boards, complete with wooden pegs. One of the carpentry work projects that summer was to finish the living room of the camp in the same decor as the Bangor House bar and coffee shop. The painting took a week or more for the oils to dry. Soon it had disappeared. I missed it.

"Dad, have you seen my painting?" I asked him.

"You wait," he tells me, "I have a surprise for you." Oh. Oh. Now what, I think.

That night he comes up from down cellar with the painting and it is framed in some of the old barn boards that he and she had gone with the trailer to get. My initials, as I was vaguely aware of signing paintings, and I was working out my artist's identity and how to sign a painting was one of my quests, my initials were partially covered up by the frame. My father, on the other hand was not contemplating the signature of an artist, had committed his act of sin uncharacteristic for this mill worker in the art world and framed my sunset, covering up my initials. I gave it to him.

"You can have it," I tell him. "You can keep the sunset."

So, for his eightieth birthday, I bought him two balloons and tied them to the cedar bush besides his headstone. I was going to get plain wishes, but his favorite grandchild, my daughter insisted we make jokes. One read, "No more birthdays, just the parties!" for the man who drank himself to death on several occasions and the other, "What hill? I don't remember any hill?" The land where he lived just down the hill from his eternal resting place. The florist asks us if we want a card to go with the balloons. "No!" We are laughing going out the door. "Are you kidding," I say, "these are going to the cemetery. He's dead. He doesn't need a card." We laugh our nervousness and irreverence. My father who's never had a balloon given to him in his life, has two floating above his grave. Waving incongruously in the wind. No card necessary. He understands. Or at least I tell myself he does.

Un mot au Sage!

*Le secret du succès dans les affaires repose dans le maintien d'une bonne réputation d'honnêteté. Tous ceux qui achètent de nous des **Pardessus d'hiver** sont prêts à nous rendre ce témoignage…Si vous avez conscience de votre intérêt vous n'acheterez pas un Pardessus ailleurs sans venir voir les bons marchés que nous offrons.*

—L'Indépendant, 4ième année, No. 2 Foi, loyauté, progrès, Fall River, Mass, 13 janvier, 1888

Chapter 45

D'une bonne réputation…
Si vous avez conscience de votre
intérêt

At least I think he understands. When we arrive at the cemetery, I notice the statue of Mary is headless. No head in sight. She has been repaired often. My brother had given her feet a bath of Portland cement when she became foot-less—broken off at the feet. Mary dissolved in a block of cement. Sure to sink if thrown into the water. I had epoxy glued her head back on one time when I discovered it was loose. Now, we find her headless. The Blessed Headless Virgin. The Silenced Woman. I think to myself, my father rages still. Still, he has the power to blast off tree branches and now, the heads of virgins. That reminds me of the restaurant—The Silent Woman. A headless woman standing there with a tray of food in the newspaper ad, circa 1970, which read:

> A Silent Woman—how can that be?
> Patient traveler do not scoff;
> Drawn from the very life is she
> and mute, because her head is off!

I remember the headless woman holding a serving tray on a carved sign in front of the restaurant on the major thoroughfare to the Belgrade Lakes region. She was there just off the highway exit.

I'm in the cemetery staring at a headless virgin—one who also served. I get afraid. I think maybe he's pissed because of the balloons. I'm defiant of my dead father. The Silenced Man. I tie the balloons to the bush anyway. We load the headless Mary, worn out by the weather, into the trunk of the car. It takes two of us to carry her, lift her into the trunk and slide her in. We take the headless virgin shopping with us to Portland. I put her in the wood pile when I get home. I remember taboos about how to burn flags when they are worn out, but what to do with religious, blessed by a priest, artifacts? What do you do with the body?

As women, of our own kind, sometimes we hold each other down so that our men, our own kind, can rape us. Character rape. A culture's inmates at war with each other. Across the gender lines battle lines are drawn. The alcoholic will not inspire any grass to grow over his tomb. Husband of my mother-in-law. She makes comment that it is all the alcohol rising to the top, killing off the grass. He was a perpetrator. Against himself and the women in his family. Secret told. What shame lies at the bottom of graves that we cannot tell them still. Was I ever a victim of silencing? First, when he beat my *maman*, when I was eight, I went to get the neighbors; they told me never to do that again, the family did. Don't ever go get the neighbors again. Second time, he beat my *maman* again; I went to get the relatives, who were not the neighbors, but lived close by. Don't ever bring shame onto us like that again the family told me. Don't ever go get anyone again. Third time, he was beating my *maman* in bed. I sent my pregnant eighteen year old sister-in-law down to break up the fight. She was staying in the house with us. She was hard to convince to take a walk…just take a walk downstairs, I pleaded with her…and he'll stop. He'll hear you walking around and he will stop hitting her. Every second counted. Big, fattened for the delivery date, she lumbered downstairs. I heard my *maman* lie. No, I'm OK. We were only talking. Fourth time, I was sixteen and running from the crazed man. He is driving a car and looking for *maman* and me walking on the street in our neighborhood. He had taken the distributor cap off the engine one more time to keep us prisoners to his anger. I had planned an escape one more time. But he came after us. In front of all my friends sitting on a porch, I decide to cross the road going in their direction for cover and safety, when he sees me, he screeches on the brakes. My *maman* yells, "Watch out!" to me. Embarrassing me in front of my friends. He is dead drunk. I turn to her. "QUIET!" "I don't want my friends to know." I am desperate to get off the streets. We go home by another route again. Only to find the house trashed. He had gone berserk and emptied all the trash cans all over the house. I dial the phone and call the police. They arrive. One of the cops who arrive is the beat cop. The one we talked to when I hung out as a teenager at the fire station up the street. All the public services were localized in the neighborhoods. Beat cops kept time with the kids in the neighborhood. He recognized me and he knew me. He wanted my *maman* to leave. To take me out of there for my own good. For the rest of my life. They pick up the reddish stained paper towels, the ones dad made at the mill when he wasn't drinking, and smelled it. "Gasoline," they say. I smell it and tell them the truth: "Lysol." He drives in. With his dog. They see him driving drunk. They ask him for his keys. He tells them the dog was driving and he is serious. "What do you want us to do?" they ask my *maman* and me. "Get the keys so we can take the car," I whisper to *maman*. "We want the keys," she boldly says. "Keep him here," I tell my friend the cop. We need to get away from him. Once more, we are not killed. We drive off to normalcy somewhere. Try to act with wholeness in a shattered world. We are shell-shocked in our existences. Cracked and bleeding under the surface. We wander and drive around all night. I practice my night driving on my permit. She sleeps in the back seat. "Go home," she tells me. "Go home." It isn't four A. M. He hasn't fried his hot dogs and onions yet. I will practice driving some more. I go home at five A.M. We walk in. The trash is gone. Picked up. The next day, he has bought me a pair of ugly, dangling earrings and a card of sorrow. To make up. I hate presents of restitution.

I am seeking the truth like confession told in reverse. The Silent Woman no more. Was I ever silent? What of the shame visited on a people, secrets at the bottom of graves, told after the long-dead have died? To whose benefit? How many years of drunkenness brought on by anger at the lack of education, the torture of an invalidated existence, clinical depression, lost directions of how to be a man, culture run amuck, the harrowing of the mill? Hollingsworth and Whitney Pulp Mills. Scott Paper Company.
Employee Number 307
Hired: February 10, 1935
Retired: (early) August 1, 1973
Seniority date: April 1, 1948
Maintenance Permanent Class 'AA' piper: December 1, 1958
Pipe Shop Permanent Class 'AAA' piper, promotion: May 30, 1960.

I counted seventeen medical Leaves of Absence. One when he was gassed by chlorine. Another electrocuted by 420 volt electricity. The man who visited the women of the men who were hurt at the mill drove into the yard and my *maman* flew out of the house. He wasn't out of his car yet. She met him in the driveway, apron hem wrapped in her hands. The sixth-grade educated man while on staging had laid hold of a pipe through which 420 voltage passed. He fainted. His partner climbed the ladder and they brought him down, into the ambulance, and to the hospital where he passed blood in his urine. After the electric shock treatments, he'd received for depression, I thought, a little more of his memory will be gone. He told us he let himself pass out or else he knew the last thing he ever did was that he'd be the ground of that voltage running through his body—dead. A piper, caught between the rail of the staging and the pipe conducting electricity. He survived. The mill sighed. They don't like to have accidents reported on their records. Safety First! Reads the board as the workers walk in each day. A record of injuries is kept. In his worker file, I found no evidence of the danger of his job. No reporting of the gassing. Or of the electrocution. Clean. File. Dates. Cold hard non-committal dates. More silence. I am the bearer of the tales.

Previous employer: Wallace Simpson, Dairy Farm, Reason for leaving: written in my *maman*'s handwriting, Betterment.

Changed mill seniority: February 10, 1935.

Jobs:

Snow Shoveler: January 2, 1935, hired

General: May 15, 1935, transferred

Yard: November 9, 1942, transferred

Truck Driver: April 23, 1945

C1B Pipers Helper: June 18, 1945

Yard Man: December 17, 1945

Truck Driver: March 10, 1946

Yard Man: November 13, 1946, displaced by Vets

C1'B' Pipers Helper: May 25, 1947

C1'A' Pipers Helper: June 1, 1947

C1 'D' Piper: April 1, 1948

C1 'C' Piper: December 20, 1948

C1 'D' Piper: February 21, 1949

Name change: From Raymond G. Côté to Gerald R. Côté, May 23, 1949

Their tombstone which he ordered after she died, depicted praying hands that she loved, pleasing her in death as he could never bring himself to in life, reads: Raymond and not Gerald, which he hated. My brother, his junior, when he read the tombstone, asked me why Raymond and not his real first name, and I told him. "Dad did that. He hates Gerald."

"I don't blame him," my older brother said. Stuck with re-run identities all of us. The oldest a junior. Mail and phone calls confused. The second named for the then fresh-dead *pépère*. The third, named in memory of a cousin who choked on corn flakes. Me, named for the twin of *maman*. The twin who had named her daughter the name of her twin. The legacy of multiple identities written on all of us as children and of the duality of cultures in negotiation for existence. The fight against foreign language living happening in English. French as the sword and the shield. The apron a signal of fierce pride at home. Flour fingerprints, greased, left on the book of life, *Better Homes and Garden Cookbook*. The sustaining graces of home cooked meals from memory. *Tourtière* as ambrosia of the Franco-Americans.

C1'C' Piper: June 1, 1949

C1 'B' Piper: June 1, 1952

C1 'A' Piper: October, 27, 1952.

I read in my father's own handwriting: Early retirement. I will receive a reduced amount of retirement annuity. Just so everyone would know. Retirement income $66.28 per month. $26.16 every 3 months, Hollingsworth and Whitney retirement. Social Security. Thirty-eight years worth of bought and paid for silence. For all of us.

Le pape vient de terminer une lettre encyclique très importante qui sera publiée très prochainement; elle se rapporte à la condition sociale de la classe ouvrière.
—*L'Indépendant*, 4ième année, No. 5 Foi, loyauté, progrès, Fall River, Mass, 3 février, 1888

Chapter 46

À la condition sociale de la classe ouvrière

A letter to *maman* and dad.

I look for what we are as members of our French culture. As women. Me and *maman*. Our lack becomes more than what it is, but at the same time you do not stop being the thing who you are. What you lack is a matter of opinion. As a Franco-American woman, I am split at the root. I learned my *maman* and her self-esteem. Highs and lows. She was poor and taunted for her poverty. Both by the school children and later on by her husband. Poverty. Shame number one. Shame number two. The lack of understanding of who we are within a context of who else doesn't understand who we are. Even those of our own culture or families. We are held accountable for an accounting. Here it is. You hold it in your hands and still, you reject its reality. The specific among the general. The genus of human types. To which family do you belong? A common question among the French. *Qui sont tes parents?* It was not until the *Côté* Family reunion held in Madawaska could we begin to put the shame behind us. That is what family reunions are all about. Previews of coming attractions. Slices of Heaven. A new-found recipe of existence. Sliced up thin. In the crowd we glimpse a man who looks so much like dad that we follow him around. He is surprised we don't speak French. Oh. Judged from within. The complications of wrinkles. How to iron it out and make yourself presentable to the public. An erring public. A public with no patience for the personal, particular, peculiar. Especially, if you are female. My father's anger and my sexuality converge and pivot on the exact same spot. It took me many years to separate myself from the root of *maman* to begin to grow a tree which casts my own shadow. I stand at the window looking out, trying to be myself—a woman. What a courageous act.

I'm concentrating on the patch and not the hole. The hole is the accusation of the nail upon the cloth. Or, the worn out places in life, rubbed to fewer and fewer threads per square inch. The rubbings, the point of getting thin-to-worn-out, the point of contact, metal against metal lacking oil to smooth the friction—those are the workings that change us. Growth happens in the patching, the covering of the holes worn upon our lives. Our understanding grows deeper

in our patching over our pains—the mystery of self-knowledge revealed in the
pin pricks of reality.

We are more our rhythms than our actuality. We replay ourselves like
records from the past—deep gouges which was set many years previous. Are
there any innocent bystanders? My father's pain was resplendent like the spec-
trum of the rainbow or as diverse as the sound waves loosed on the universe.
What he failed to realize in venting, re-exposing, lamenting, howling about his
wounds—expecting us to lick them—was that he was not the only one to have
suffered life and living. My *maman* also had an unhappy and unfortunate life. She,
too suffered in her youth—not just him—but she was not going to make us all
pay for her pain. He had his excuses. Those of us still alive are reeling from the
incidents which took place in our youth. Do I understand the incidence of that
much evil in a man toward a women with whom he made four children? I do not.
The need for control, power, definition, exercising the grip on another's life.
Can I answer the question about why my father deliberately treated my *maman*
and the children so badly? And intermittently, being kind as well. No. I cannot.
I can only guess.

My *maman* was a 'good woman' as my father used to say to compliment
other men's wives. "I'm a 'good woman' too," *maman* would reply. Self-affirming.
She, unfortunately, made a bad choice. Of husband. She always loved God
throughout her ordeal—the cruelty and hardship of her life—but she wondered
about God and his seemingly unarbitrary selection for punishment. I think she
wondered what, just exactly, were God's standards? She argued with God often
and she questioned who God chose to reward with what she understood to be
a good life. She sought immediate gratification alleviating her of her personal
pain or cross. She had duped herself and married a crucifixion. A personal nail-
ing to the cross and he thought he was her husband. I've been all over this with
a fine toothed comb. To write it on paper does not give the breadth, width or
depth of meaning attached to the words. The man was not all monster, but he
was a fearful presence. Always hurting her when he was drunk. Dangerous. And
when sober, a mixture of manliness. Always domineering, but they had some
semblance of healthiness in their relationship. I can see him, but I see him multi-
faceted, many cuts to the stone, many gouges.

Groupes Canadiens des États-Unis——Une partie de nos chantres se proposent d'aller chanter la messe à Indian Orchard dimanche prochain
——L'Indépendant, 4ième année, No. 2 Foi, loyauté, progrès, Fall River, Mass, 13 janvier, 1888

Chapter 47

Une partie de nos chantres se proposent d'aller chanter

I'm washing the family laundry in public. It is a wonder why do I do such a thing. Very cautiously I unwrap the freshly laundered image of the family. The cultural family living in a five-tier layer cake town by the great river Kennebec in memory of a spirit long-lived. A geography of explanation, not accusation. Generation upon generation of immigrants coming and going upon a piece of historical multi-layered riverbanks rippling from the shock of their entry. A class of people thrown into a town. A town set upon itself to deny most of them and their existence. What profit is there in telling the shame? What shame? The one you cannot erase from your ancestry. And on top of that, we are proud to be who we are. Proud to be French.

What is so pointed in the local news as a murder trial between ethnics? Or the deaths of several old women in a place where they are not valued? What are the crimes of self-hate committed on a people, who have the gun of self-destruction placed in their hands deemed unholy or unworthy? Who commits the hate? Self or Other? What of a husband's drunken ranting over-worked, tired, and debased on a daily basis? What scourge of centuries old shame visits the children's children? What source of healing? Of remembering? Of self-knowing? What of the accented speech? What of the gesturing while speaking? What of the mental wards overfull with patients speaking in tongues? What of the pill-pushing in decipherment?

February 19, 1982

He has severe, chronic, obstructive pulmonary disease. The condition is worsening.

February 22, 1982

I have reviewed the above employee's medical records and agree that this man's condition is worsening.

Beyond a single family story lies the whole town at its doorstep. One does not get sick and die in a vacuum, only in neglect. Neglect of understanding. Or remembering. Or no place to be. She had no recourse as well. Shelters were non-existent. Self-help a mode of guaranteeing poverty after a lifetime of co-pounding in nails into the house they had built. The allegory of a couple as a stand-in for the struggles of their French-in-Maine family. Some would deny the heartache existed. Too close to the bone. Some would say rejection was not their experience. Nor the abuse. Neither the venting. They are probably right. On the money. With change coming back to them as well. Some managed to live free and die happy. Those are the ones *maman* envied. The happy marriages. The happy culture types. The happy French. The ones where the woman *was porté sur le mains*. Pampered. Spoiled. Pleased. "Everyone is not like us," she said.

Maman died not knowing happiness for herself. Many in the Franco-American culture die never knowing their belonging or the possible happiness of the marriage of their souls to their heritage. The daily battles of designing an existence of duality, the masks for the public and the make-up for the private like the masks of Tragedy and Comedy exchanging places forever. The inside, turned-out story of a group of people. Each with families and individuals included. Tossed about on the sea of being alive. How do you tell the story of an entire group without leaving anyone out or by telling my version and not my brothers' or to relate that our men do sometimes make love to us and then black our eyes. Shame of the Fork in the Lunch Basket Existence.

Blame. Blame. Blame. I'm sick of it. I want to tell a story of an open-minded society that welcomes with open minds. That's what we are here for, to live with the knowledge of ourselves and to anticipate spices. Recipes of success. Troubles, sure. Everybody's got them, but we are into our winter of healing. I see the spirit of peace moving on the land as the air moves over the tall grasses. Wheat sheaves before the harvest in golden glory. Bread of our daily beginning anew in ourselves in the company of many others. The story of a group of French-speaking people who came to Maine to work in the mills. There is richness. Texture in the story. Weavings of pride in belonging because we came here and we live here. Healing in the next generations of the sores and pains of our *maman*s and dads, *mémères* and *pépères*. I remember the lessons of sewing that the needle taught me about life. The eyes in my fingers guide the thread to the button holes. Those not able to see, feel. I know the rhythms that make me a member of the group of Franco-Americans. I am the girl of the riverbank. I am the one who writes her *maman* to freedom beyond the confines of the grave and the living. I am the *maman*. I am the quilt maker of story upon the bed of life. I am the remade patch upon the hole of living. I will not fall into the trap of believing myself unworthy to write myself and my *maman* and others. I will speak the story of the land upon which the family dwells still. Despite the hardships. Despite the measures in society that says I don't belong because I'm not like *les Améritchaines*, whoever they are. The Dominant Culture. The prescribed way of being. New York cool and the overbearing definition of accepted people passing judgment or worse, ignoring their community. I am of the riverbank and of the pride in the fight against being erased. Women of the culture may not agree. Some are too delicate in their lives to be anything but pure and holy. That's good for them. Others, fell to the demands that they become whores. Or, simply judged by their geographically attached sexual selves. They live their version of themselves. My *maman* fought for her definition of herself. I fight for mine. Sometimes we fight for who we are against our own men of our own culture. The men have to control something in the pecking order. So their fists of rage come crashing down on the women. And some women of our culture hold down our own women in the fight for expression of who we are. The cultural men and the cultural women. Together. Sometimes, gentling is the response, but often, the harsh conditions of the larger picture demands an exact payment of soul for freedom to be someone you are not for your entire life. A loss of people on the plains. Who would tell me otherwise?

BUANDERIE DE FALL RIVER! FALL RIVER LAUNDRY, No. 24, rue Hartwell, Collette et manchettes, 2 cents, pièce tapis battus et nettoyés à la vapeur, 4 cents la verge. Linge lavé, empesé, repassé ou non, au grès des clients. On va chercher sans frais tous les paquets à domicile...

—*L'Indépendant*, 4ième année, No. 3 Foi, loyauté, progrès, Fall River, Mass, 20 janvier, 1888

Chapter 48

Collette et manchettes, 2 cents

Perfect, present, future tense. In French. Everything in French. Even if it is in English, it is still in French. A layer of French living laid over by layers of popular culture or popular culture covered by living done in French. Intertwined. I wish I had a happier story to tell, but I've made my peace with its ugliness. It is a truthful, unpretty face. I have learned to love the story I hated. One of the deep reverberations that I must reacquaint myself with. Legends. Customs. Recipes. Folktales. Stories. Songs. Futuristic visions. I have visions of perfect, present, future tense. What am I in the future of my Franco-American womaning? Do I learn the language? Do I write my way to freedom? Will I be understood by even myself, I wonder, let alone someone without a cultural blueprint. I am scared. Afraid of the outcome. The judgments. The pronouncements. Some have more of the inner sanctum secret passwords than others. Some have the original recipes. Some can sing. Some know the essence of the moment told in French words. I can hear the heart beat of *Québec*. I can hear the St. Lawrence River, *le fleuve St. Laurent* running in my blood stream. I am giant and I have out of the body experiences picking up tankers on the St. Lawrence looking down from the 13th floor of *Le Concorde*. I eat the soup, bread, *plat principal*, and desert without a bit of explanation necessary. I climb on my knees the prayer stairs at *Ste. Anne de Beaupré*. I am close to *Jean Côté's* grave on *l'Île d'Orléans*. He arrived just yesterday—1600 something. I married the very distant cousin. I eat the soup. I bake the bread. I am a *couseuse*. I make bold the colors in my house. I get dizzy admiring the roofs in *Québec*. The colors on the houses leave me breathless. I have been shamed to white, but I vow to return to the palette of true colors. I dream the visions of young women in French. Equanimity in the cultural unearthing of their legacy of the near millennium. Do-it-to-yourself archeology. The cookbook of life rendered for what it is. That which sustains the generations to come. Pride, not shame in the female cook pot. Modern day tapestry of living unparalleled in its boasts. *On parle français, ici* the commercial advertisements read. Understood, at last.

I talk about losing a piece of one's body and it is like losing a piece of one's self in their culture. Changed forever, but you continue to live just the same. You take it all in stride. I chose to tattoo pressed flowers over my mastectomy scar. Just like in the poster made famous by the woman depicting the female crucifixion, salvation for all, in the skyline pose. Naked to the waist, outdoors and celebrating single-breastedness. Culture women, Franco-American women, in the folds of nature and the future, celebrating the newly designed and defined selves. That present, future, tense. Maybe, not perfect, but who would want it?

Am I willing to give more weight to the dark side of story rather than the good side of story—although the dark is as necessary as the light. My fears are what intrude. Because in each story is the light and the dark. The evil and the good.

I want to tell someone something and one day I need to tell it from over here with that day's rations of embellishments, and then the next day I have a different view of what I want to say about the same thing because I've changed and I've become better seasoned in my own passage through the personal truths. I can understand the event in a different light. I am impressed with what I choose to tell and what I choose to not tell and then when I tell the story, how it sometimes doesn't even come close to what it is I experienced or what happened. Words are slippery. Slimy. Gooey. Slick. Silky. A breath of air on the wind. Utterances echoing. I am struck with what a story is about. (The Franco-American and Acadian festivals in the summer whispering our fame.) Usually not what actually took place because people have a way of not corroborating their stories. (Everyone's recipe for *tourtière* is different.) They need to tell their version to protect their interests. (Stewed tomatoes as signature.) Or, they just cannot tell a good story or put the right words to the experience. (Immigration as person denied in a land of forget who you were, you're here now story.) Whoever they are writing or telling the story to does not have the time or the patience to listen to them. They tell the long version when a shorter version could be said. (How do you spell your name mill boss says to M. *Poulin*, the non-reader and non-writer. P-O-O-L-E-R, the mill boss tells him.)

When you draw it is a matter of seeing more than a matter of moving the pencil or charcoal to do what you want. Some skill of the hand is needed to record the seeing, but it is in the seeing the thing drawn is recorded. The event of a tree standing there in all its glory of autumn. The river coming into focus for the duration of the winter months as the leaves shed their camouflage and the river's disappearing act in the Spring of the year when the trees regain their composure of leaves once again. (Reclaiming one's right to one's culture and singing one's songs. The forces of tradition blowing against the shores of modernity. What flashes across your mind is the view of dancers dancing the gigues while you shop the aisles in the grocery store. The women all around you speak in French or *Franglais*. They say the French culture is dead. Are these people ghosts?) Regeneration. The sign of nature to us that we too are hopefuls in possibilities of becoming new people.

To write, is to see. To record. To believe in the belonging to the telling. To express. To explain. (Even if only to oneself.) Acquire. Words are paint. Words as picture. Dad always said "one picture is worth a thousand words." It is only one picture and a thousand words are a thousand words with the possibility of multiplication, proliferation, exponential growth because of their suggestive lucidity.

So we tell and re-tell. Telling has nothing to do with competing. Or being beat down because the telling does not match a criteria of some other kind of telling. (*No Adam in Eden* by Grace Metalious or *Canuck* by *Camille Lessard Bissonnette* telling.) Telling is its own story and its own reward. The story has its birth in our way of being and not to doubt our experience just because someone has a formula for themselves and their story. My story is of me as I represent the *grandmères'* bloodline. (Raining down through the centuries like crashing waves of consciousness coming to being. When I walked the streets of Angers, France I did not know that the woman immigrant who began the line of women on my *maman*'s side lived here centuries before.)

Like I can remember the curve in the road which I can see from my windows in my house with all the years I've looked out onto the road with my thoughts. Thinking of my *maman*'s death, my father's death, the years of traffic going by, the seasons changing under my gaze, the steeples visible in the distance, my children, my brothers' and their lives. My brother's death. Me, as a young *maman*, as a cancer patient, with my husband coming home on that road. The train tracks which cross the road's path. The yellow lines newly painted and fading with the passing time and traffic. I stand in the house and the road has not moved or changed, but yet I see the road very differently now than when I first lived here with my hopes set on high. Sorry, but that is not the way the bend in the road goes. The road is resolute and real. (One million *Québécois* immigrated to the Northeast United States between the years 1820 and 1920 all with descendants today living in the entire Northeast.) It is me standing at the window looking at its curve imposing my meaning on the view. My thoughts floating heavenward, becoming golden letters in the book of life.

Like the heartbeat, no matter what, passed on from generation to generation. I have the French language and the French way of being in Maine. A historical me. One who was born into a life. Lives. Moving toward the white light that sucks up the soul. We are full of smells in our souls of those things which we live with in our lifetimes. That is why our sense of smell is so acute. Like our eyes which are windows into our soul, our sense of smell is how we find our way home. (The frenzied supper hour. The salt-porked beans.) Our five senses are like the petals of a star in the heavens, or a star fish on the beach, or the inside of an apple cut to reveal its inner heart's core of truth star. Our own five-pointed starness of head and limbs echo the central being of unity to which we all belong in relation to the other five-pointed beings and their placement. Their constancy of change in the sky. Who we are when we move together. The five senses are our points of being inside of the other physically five appendages. We are all stars. All *vedettes*. In our own universes. We are entities and parts of constellations.

Living does a little twisty dance all over expectations and the story changes from the one you have in your head. (I will be French in Maine, Franco-American female, and proud of it.) So it all becomes more story. Or song. Lamentations. War wounds. Epitaph. What we choose to see when we look is what is really there—disappointment and celebration. We can remain aloof, outside, cold, indifferent; or we can belong, praise, recognize, sing alleluias. We can reject. Accept at will. Disagree with. Affirm. We belong to the story plane much like we belong to the picture plane. Depth of field and focus. Good lighting. Bad lighting. Shadow. Sun. Dark. The shifting sands of conversing. Telling. Storying. Each one comes to us and we are filters of the future. We decide what will be seen and heard only so much as we carefully choose the words which do the telling.

For someone to doubt the telling or to devalue the telling of a story makes telling difficult for the one doing story. And also for the one who refuses a story's life. Clear, careful, concise. Clean. With a mind to multiple views of the same view. And the passing years. That is how we tell a story. That is how we become future.

Fin

About the author

Côté Robbins was brought up bilingually in a Franco-American neighbor-hood in Waterville, Maine known as 'down the Plains'. Her *maman* came from Wallagrass, a town in the northern part of the state of Maine and her father was from Waterville. She has spent many years researching the origins and visiting the hometowns of her ancestors in Canada and France.

Côté Robbins was the winner of the Maine Chapbook Award for her work of creative nonfiction entitled, *Wednesday's Child*. She is a founder and Executive Director of the Franco-American Women's Institute. She is currently working on a sequel titled, *If These Walls Could Talk*. She has edited the volume, *Canuck and Other Stories*, a translation of early Franco-American women writers. You can find information on these books at http://www.rhetapress.com.

She lives in Brewer with her husband, David.

CPSIA information can be obtained at www.ICGtesting.com
Printed in the USA
LVOW13s1649201113

362109LV00004B/715/P